THE
SHIPCARVER'S
HANDBOOK

THE
SHIPCARVER'S
HANDBOOK

How to Design and Execute Traditional Marine Carvings

Jay S. Hanna

WoodenBoat Publications, Inc.
1988

Again—to the other Urchin.

Published by WoodenBoat Publications, Inc.
Brooklin, Maine 04616
Copyright 1988 by Jay S. Hanna
All rights reserved.
ISBN 0-937822-14-0
Library of Congress Catalog Card Number: 88-5762

Hanna, Jay S.
    The shipcarver's handbook.
    Rev. ed. of: Marine carving handbook. © 1975.
    1. Ship decoration.   2. Wood-carving. I. Hanna,
Jay S.   Marine carving handbook. II. Title.
VM308.H35   1988   736.4   88-5762
ISBN 0-937822-14-0.

Acknowledgments

For the help and professionalism that changed a few words, drawings, and photographs into this book, I wish to thank Peter Spectre, Kathleen Brandes, Rodney Robertson, and the good people of *WoodenBoat*—Jane Crosen for her editing, Sherry Streeter for the layout, and Jon Wilson for his faith and enthusiasm. How nice to have friends who do their jobs superbly!

My thanks also to the woodcarvers and photographers who allowed me the use of their material for illustrations.

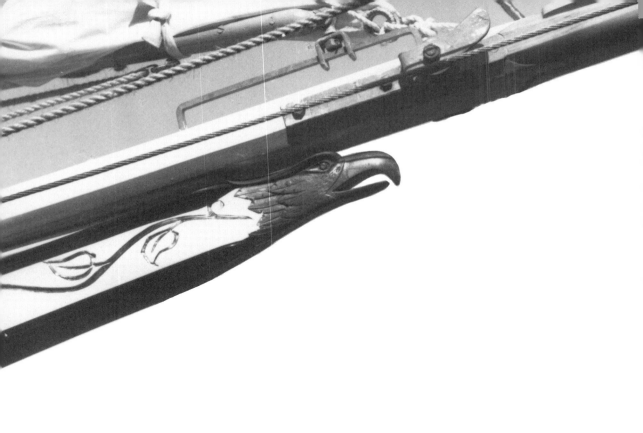

Contents

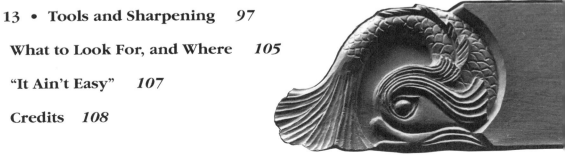

Publisher's Preface

When the original edition of this book was published as the *Marine Carving Handbook* in 1975, it was welcomed as the first thorough approach to the methods used in marine carving. Although there had been several studies of the various works of shipcarvers through history, there were none that focused on the techniques involved. The result had been that, although professional woodcarvers could execute a variety of carvings in the marine vernacular, the subtleties of the art were at risk of disappearing, and there was little guidance available for the aspiring amateur. Jay Hanna's *Handbook* appeared just in time. For years it proved to be a very popular book, going through several printings. But, a few years ago, the publisher decided that it had to let the book go out of print.

Jay Hanna knew that the book could benefit from some revising and expanding, and he decided to explore these options with WoodenBoat Publications. With our common interest in improving the content and design of the book, WoodenBoat was only too happy to participate in keeping this classic work alive. Working together with Jay, we proceeded to expand the text and increase the number of illustrations. At the same time, we redesigned the format of the book so that techniques were more clearly described for readers. The result is a happy blend of old and new material in a fresh and open format.

The art of marine carving is almost as old as boats and ships themselves. From the most primitive figureheads to the most elaborate sterncastle carvings, sailors and shipbuilders alike have taken these embellishments very seriously, and the shipcarvers have left us with a deep and rich tradition. Maritime museums around the world boast wonderful and inspiring examples of the shipcarver's art, in all its elaborate and intricate glory. But there is little call for such work anymore; today we work with less complex themes, carved with grace and elegant simplicity.

The Shipcarver's Handbook is a guide to carving a variety of decorative items—for both boat and home—from a simple nameboard to a proud eagle, and doing so with confidence. In a style that is warm, wise, and patient, Jay Hanna gently urges the reader along. He is a man who loves the shipcarver's traditions, and who is happy to share his knowledge of these traditions. His discussions of the all-important aesthetic considerations in the *design* of carvings are as practical as his recommendations on woods and tools. His descriptions of technique lead the reader carefully through the steps for executing such things as trailboards, billetheads, and banners. The carving of dolphins, stars, and rope borders is also discussed, and the reader is encouraged to create his or her own designs for imaginative carvings. Drawings with grids are provided throughout the book as guides to carving at larger scales, and include three different simple alphabets. For those who need it, a section on sources for tools and woods is provided, as are notes on obtaining full-sized patterns for some of the carvings shown in the book.

Jay Hanna knows well the gratification that results from practicing the arts of marine carving, and we are fortunate, indeed, that he has chosen to share his knowledge and experience.

Jonathan Wilson
Editor, *WoodenBoat* Magazine

THE
SHIPCARVER'S
HANDBOOK

1 • An Old and Honored Art

Among the joys and frustrations that come to anyone running a one-man shop, and doing the same work for money that others sometimes do for a hobby, are the continual letters and visits from people seeking advice—and my shop has been no exception. It cuts into the working time for which I can bill, and thus reduces my income, but I must admit to the double pleasure of meeting some very nice people and feeling flattered to have my opinion sought. Many times, the questions asked have no definitive answer without a demonstration followed by practice on the learner's part, and my shop isn't set up for teaching. Besides, I dislike having other people use my tools; they get used to the way I handle them and don't take kindly to anyone else giving them directions.

So, this book is for all you good people who want to try carving decorations in a traditional marine style for your boat or house. There's nothing here about wood sculpture, soap carving, or linoleum-block cutting—just traditional marine carving. Enjoy yourself!

Someone once wrote that the art of shipcarving is dead. Don't you believe it! It may be old and is surely tottering around with a cane, but it is kept alive by small injections of enthusiasm and skill from professionals and amateurs alike. It would be hard, these days, to find a William Rush, a John or Simeon Skillin, or a Samuel McIntire—four of the many highly skilled men who carved life-sized figures to grace the bows of ships in the late 1700s and early 1800s. But there's always someone around to do what little carving is needed. That might be someone who earns part of his living at it, like me, or someone who wants the satisfaction of doing it himself, like you. No one, let alone me, can put down words that will make you a master carver, but this book can help you get started on the right heading, and perhaps it will keep you away from some of the shoals.

Shipcarving is an old and honored art. The addition of decorative carvings

1 • **An elaborately carved stern of the 18th century.**

to vessels reached a peak of absurdity in the 1600s and 1700s. Why were the ships of that time loaded down with so much nonfunctional art? Partly because of pride in the vessel and to "show the flag" with great grandeur, but partly also for the same reason that Detroit puts chrome and racing stripes on a new car: to sell the product. Naval architects and yard owners had to sell a new design to an admiralty board, most of whose members didn't know the pointy end of a ship from the other end. If the model were covered with carvings (Figure 1), they could understand some of what they were buying and were more likely to appropriate the money for the whole.

By the time of the clipper ships in the 1850s, hull designs had been cleaned up and simplified, and the great head structure and its bracing were gone— and with it, the quarter galleries and multi-decked sterns. Without all this structure to decorate, and with an eye to the dollar (remember, these were merchant vessels, not Navy ships; they had to earn their way), designers reduced the carvings to a simple few: a life-sized figure with a carved scroll to rest on in the bow (see Figure 2), and perhaps an eagle on the transom. Pride of ownership kept this much decoration; besides, it was good advertising.

Shipbuilding and ship design constitute a traditional art, and even though our own vessels are pretty small today and most can only be classed as boats, we do like to carry on the tradition and have some carving on them. What lady isn't more attractive with a little decoration?

There are no descriptions of how to carve a life-sized figurehead in this book. Few of us could use a figurehead on our boats; besides, I've never carved one. We will concentrate on what can be used—billetheads, trailboards, quarter boards, and stern decorations. If you have the money and no interest or desire to butcher a piece of nice wood, there are carvers who will design and execute what you need. Look well and critically at their past work, because carvers, like any other breed, come with good, poor, and in-between abilities. Decide on the one who does the type of work you enjoy. I do hope, however, that you'll try doing your own carving. It's a pleasurable occupation if you've been sitting in an office all day making those important decisions that keep the company, or the country, running. You may cut a finger or take a chip out where you want it in, but a little cussing, some glue, or a Band-Aid usually keeps things rolling. Carving helps to fill in those long winter evenings, and it keeps your thoughts of summer cruising active. Besides, in the spring you can do a little chest-expanding to your admiring fellow boatmen.

To enlarge the design drawings in this book, you may use the squared spacing method (increase the size of the squares, and redraw the design proportionately); an easier way is to use an enlarging photocopier (or have an enlargement made by a photocopying service). I hope you'll also venture to

2 • Figurehead of the American clipper *America*, carved in 1974 by the Herbert Gleason firm. The lady's head was copied from a U.S. silver dollar.

create your own designs, because the real enjoyment comes from seeing your own ideas in three dimensions.

Most courses in manual skills require that the student make many practice cuts, lines, and what-have-you before attempting anything that could be called a finished product. Now, I haven't anything against this system for the other fellow, but I get bored making a whole series of practice anythings. I've been told that I wanted to be a Michelangelo the first time out; the truth is, I think most of us would prefer to have something to show for our labors. Then, too, assuming that you are perhaps willing to scrap your first efforts if the final results are poor, it's better practice to work on an actual piece, the design of which demands more discipline in your cuts.

2 · Woods for Marine Carving

The woods you use for carving are like boat designs—they are all a compromise. You want the wood to be soft so it will be easy to carve, but you also want it to be hard so it will resist wear and breakage. I'll give some of the pros and cons, and you pick what you want to work with—the only real limitations being availability, cost, and what you are going to carve.

The usual rule is: The finer the detail, the closer the grain and the harder the wood. Reading books on general carving (i.e., furniture, decorative interior woodwork, and sculpture) won't guide us too well for marine work. In furniture carving, wood colors and grain figuring are very critical, but we will encounter little of that. Most marine carvings are painted or gilded; carvings that are left natural are usually of a classic marine wood, such as mahogany or teak. Small, intricate detail in a carving requires holly, lime, pear, or other fine-grained, dense wood; but you won't, I hope, be doing anything that fine on a trailboard that's going to be seen from 6 feet or more away! When you make a model of your boat, and that trailboard and its carving get reduced to an inch or so long, that's the time to use pear and some engraving tools.

The general rule is simply this: The softer the wood (barring balsa, which is useless in carving), the easier it is on your muscles. Balancing this, the harder and more close-grained the wood, the sharper and crisper you can carve details, and the better the carving will resist abuse and aging. Straight-grained wood is, of course, the best. It's hard enough, at first, to get the tools to do what you want them to do without fighting twisty grains and knots.

However, there was a novel about clipper ships that I vaguely remember reading many years ago, in which a carver selected the wood for a full-sized woman's figure to grace the bow of a new vessel. He took great care in picking over the pile of logs, and his sense of spatial relationships must have been extraordinary. The finished figure (a similar one is shown in Figure 3) was undraped to the waist, as was customary, but what was unusual was that a knot with its circular surrounding grain formed each nipple. If you can pick wood this cleverly, go to it!

For the rest of us, clear white pine, with its relatively mild grain, is an ideal wood to begin carving with. It cuts easily; and it's so soft, you'll have to watch yourself to keep from cutting off too much. It's good to begin with a wood that you have to be careful with, as this trains your hands to move the tool only where you want it to cut.

Basswood has always been known as a modelmaker's wood, primarily because it is usually clear and straight-grained. It is soft and hasn't much strength, but it does very well for painted boards with carved-in letters. Another nice thing about it (at least, at the time of this writing) is that it costs half as much as pine does.

Mahogany is a little harder to carve, but for giving a rich look to that finished nameboard, it certainly beats painted pine. If you can find it, get Honduras mahogany because of its straight, even grain. But look at a piece of Philippine mahogany: its grain pattern, composed of belts 1/2 inch wide, tends to go up in one belt and down in the next, making carving with the grain a game of musical chairs. It can be carved, of course, but unless you have a good vocabulary of cuss words, don't use it as a beginning wood.

And so we come to teak, the best wood to use around the water. If you need much of it, fill your pockets with gold before going to the lumberyard. In spite of the fact that teak will take the edge off a circular-saw blade, it isn't all that hard to carve. You'll have to sharpen your tools more frequently because the abrasive in teak has a great dulling ability, but the wood carves beautifully. It is, however, quite brittle, and it's very easy for a short-grained piece to break off. With care, sharp tools, and, of course, that skill you're going to acquire, you can handle it.

The great English carving wood, for architectural purposes, was oak. American oak comes in two kinds—red and white. Red is the softer variety, quite brittle and not resistant to decay from dampness. White oak is preferred for marine use. It is very hard—your tools must be sharp, your arm stout, and your patience of goodly amount to work with white oak—but the end result is beautiful.

Most suppliers of boat lumber can sell you short ends and blocks that are ideal for carving projects. If you have the time and inclination, you can collect your own storehouse of wood for future projects. Poking around some of the smaller mills, you can sometimes find green pieces that later will be great stuff to carve. The large mills usually have no time for special wood unless you order it by the carload, but the small operator is more apt to be obliging and keep his eye out for clear stock for you and set it aside. Wood bought this way has to be stacked in a well-ventilated, dry place, with sticking between planks for good air circulation. The rough rule for drying lumber is a year for each inch of thickness. Collecting good wood for carving can become a hobby in itself—so much so that you can find yourself not wanting to cut into any of your stock, each piece seemingly "too good" to use for the job at hand. (Whole books have been written on the subject of woods for carving; see "What to Look For, and Where" at the back of this book.)

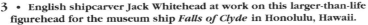

3 • English shipcarver Jack Whitehead at work on this larger-than-life figurehead for the museum ship *Falls of Clyde* in Honolulu, Hawaii.

3 • First Tools and a First Project

W oodcarving tools come in dozens of shapes and sizes, and if you have enough money, you can easily go out and buy sets that will be the envy of us all. With this abundance of riches, you will find that most of the tools will be like money in cold storage—seldom used, but there when needed. Really, very few tools are needed to start with, and you can add to them as your interest increases.

Don't be conned into buying sets of small, short-handled "carving tools." These are great for linoleum-block cutting, but not for the kind of carving we're going to do. What you need are tools that are long enough to get both hands on for control, and these are usually known as "professional" carving tools.

Be sure also that you buy "shouldered" tools. The shoulder is a swelling in the shank that prevents the tool from being forced deeper and deeper into the handle when the tool gets pushed hard or hit with a mallet.

---

4 • A nameboard with simple "feather" ends, each with a land for a screw. This is a quarter board's traditional proportions.

Instead of listing pages of tools at this point and scaring you with their variants and cost, I'll just go ahead with carving something, and show you what you need for that job. If we start with a traditional bow or quarter nameboard (such as in Figure 4) that you can use on your boat or your house, you can do the whole thing with three or four tools that won't put you in debt to some friendly loan office.

The first tool is a knife. Yes, a knife—and it can be used for more than crudely carving a heart and initials on the old apple tree. Not, however, a jackknife with a folding blade; it's prone to folding with your finger between the blade and the handle, and the resulting bloodstains spoil the work. A sloyd (an all-purpose knife with a short, fine, fixed blade, like the one shown in Figure 9) will do for most uses. With this tool alone you can carve a quarter board. To make the work go more quickly, you can add a 1/2-inch chisel or a skew chisel, a V-gouge (parting tool), and a hand-fret saw (if you don't own a scroll saw or bandsaw). You don't *need* these tools (most of which are illustrated in Figure 86), but they will lessen the effort expended.

Lettering and Design

No work that you do will be better than your layout, particularly the lettering. Why people will spend hours carving something with loving care, but not spend the initial time making a good design, I'll never know. Maybe they are too anxious to get started, but it's a long way back when the finished piece is spoiled by a poor appearance. A misspelled word can easily be corrected on the drawing, but I've never been able to get an eraser to work on a carved letter. Poor-looking nameboards are usually at fault in the size and spacing of the letters, so take your time before you go digging holes in a good piece of wood.

Figures 5 and 6 are examples of some alphabets that can be used for carving, beginning with the basic block letters demanded by officialdom for registry—in Maine, required to be a minimum of 3 inches high. Because block letters are simple to carve, easy to read, and have a long history of marine use,

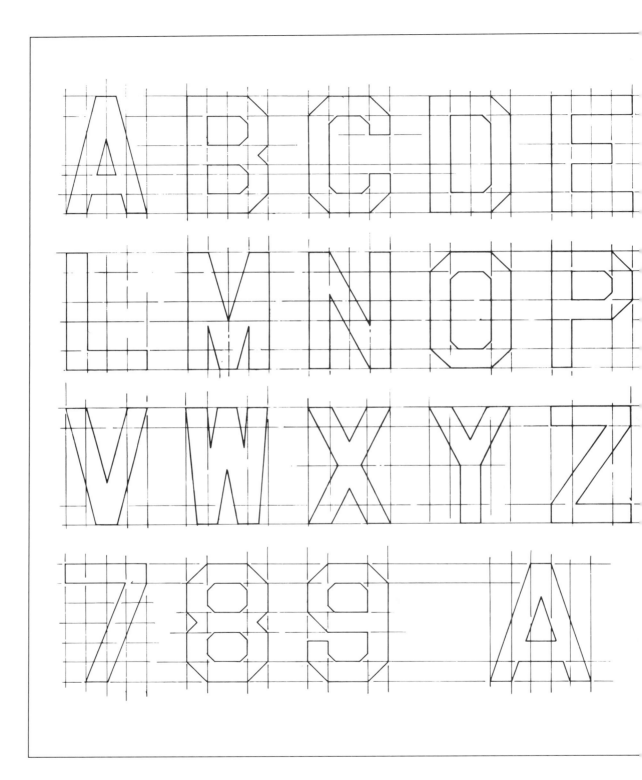

10

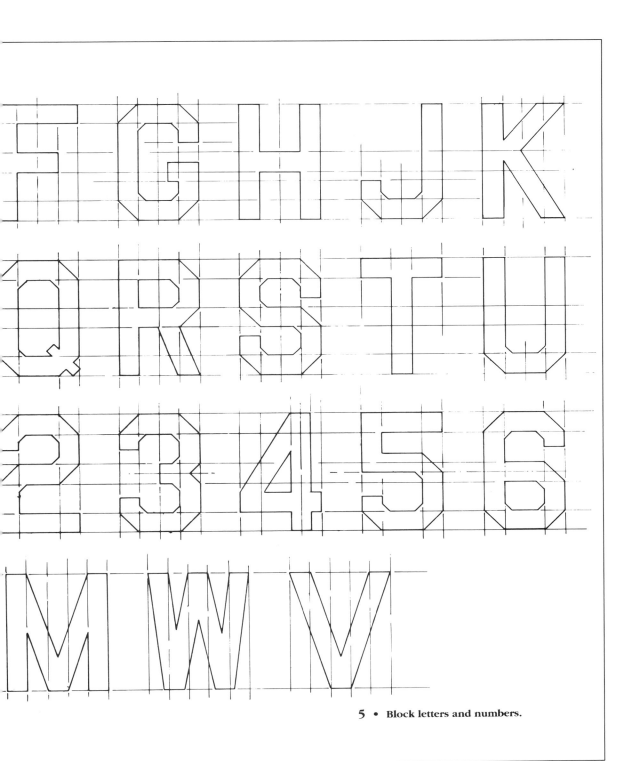

5 • **Block letters and numbers.**

ABCDEFG
NOPQRST

ABCDEFGHI
PQRSTUVW

they make a good choice for a first project. Another attraction of block letters, for the beginner, is that they can be carved with the minimum of tools—a knife, a straight chisel, or a skew chisel.

If you examine the block-letter alphabet (Figure 5), you'll notice that all the letters and numbers are the same width and height. You can follow this and be "correct" if you want to, but I've included substitutes for A, M, W, and V that are one stroke wider. They're easier to read, and pleasanter to look at.

H I J K L M
U V W X Y Z

J K L M N O
X Y Z

6 • Simple serif alphabets.

Good lettering has many variations, and as you get away from the block style, you will become more aware of letter spacing and style combinations that look right. The goal is to achieve a balance between letters and spacing so that words "read well." For example, if you have two straight-sided letters next to each other, such as H and N, the distance between them should be greater than that between two O's; it's the total area of white space separating the letters that counts, not the lineal distance. Later on, when you use letter-

WOODCARVER

7 • Varying the height of rounded letters.

---

ing styles other than the rectangular block form, you will find that, by extending rounded letters (such as O and S) slightly above and/or below the guidelines, as in Figure 7, you can make them appear to be the same height as the flat-topped letters. The design and layout of lettering is a craft all in itself, and I suggest that if you are interested, you check your library for books on the subject. Also helpful are the catalogs of pressure lettering (Letraset) and type styles used by graphic artists. These catalogs may be found at art supply stores.

Back to our project. First, I suggest that you enlarge the letters you need from the designs in this book—either by drawing them freehand, if you're handy with a pencil, or by using an enlarging photocopier. Cut out squares of

---

8 • Letters slanting forward at the bow, vertical on the quarter boards at the stern.

the paper, each containing one letter, so that you can arrange them on a background sheet (ordinary plain white shelf paper works well). Back and fill with them until the spacing looks good—nothing cramped, and no wide-open gaps—and stick them down temporarily with small pieces of clear tape. View the lettering from across the room; squinting helps you see the balance between the letters and the white spaces, especially if you have colored in the letters with a crayon or felt-tipped marker. Remember, most viewing of the nameboard will be from a distance. For this reason, lettering should be in a simple style and somewhat bold so that it will be legible. (If you are operating a rumrunner or other illegal craft, use Old English lettering—or German Gothic, which is almost impossible to figure out.) When you're happy with the arrangement, cover the layout with tracing paper and make a complete drawing.

Lettering on the old sailing ships was sometimes slanted to fit the lines of the vessel (Figure 8); lettering on the bow would slant forward, paralleling the stem rabbet line, whereas quarter boards usually had vertical lettering. Because the space they were made to fit was narrow, most letters were quite wide for their height so that the name stretched along the sheer. If you want to be traditional, follow these proportions; nothing looks worse than a nameboard that's shaped like the cover of a shoe box.

Nameboard end decorations can be as simple or as elaborate as you wish. A simplified traditional "feather" end with a land for a screw fastening is

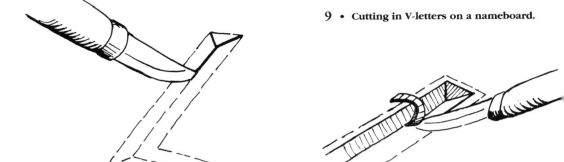

a   b

shown in Figures 4 and 7. In the design provided (Figure 12), the squares are 1/4-inch divisions, but they can be enlarged to any size, depending on the width you want. Use your imagination if you prefer something different; another variation of the feather end is shown in Figure 15.

Get your hands on a nice, clear, dry piece of white pine or basswood at your local pattern or cabinet shop—about 5/8 inch thick for a small board, 3/4 inch thick for anything longer than 2 feet. Have it planed to thickness and cut to the width you want.

Tape your board end-decoration drawing to your lettering layout, leaving enough spacing between the end letters and design to avoid confusion—at least one letter space at the minimum; more is better. Transfer your artwork with carbon paper (use a sharp pencil, but don't dig in with it), and be sure to go over all the lines.

If you are going to finish your board bright, it might help to stain the surface before laying out the letters. This way, every cut that meets the surface has a definite line between light and dark wood. Conversely, if the board is to be painted, you could white-prime the face. Your layout lines will show up well and so will all cut edges.

Setting Up

There are a few requirements for making carving a pleasure. I would say that you must stand to work effectively, but that's one of those dogmatic statements that some neat character is always proving wrong, so let's just say that it's easier to carve standing up. (That allows me to go on admiring those people who have to sit, and still do nice work.) I think I can be right and say

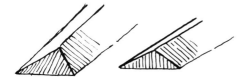 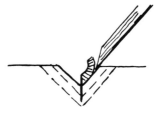

c   d

that it would be hard to do good work on a flimsy card table, so another requirement is a firm, rugged bench anchored to the floor with bolts (or weighted down with a big rock on its bottom shelf). When you begin getting enthusiastic with a mallet and chisel on white oak, something is going to give, and you don't want it to be your bench.

One thing that pertains to all your carving work is lighting. Carving at a bench with the light directly overhead will flatten out the cuts. Have the light coming in from the side to make the shadows show all unevenness. What looks good under an overhead light can be embarrassing when seen on edge in the sunlight.

A word here about sharpness. The most useless tool in the world is a dull one. So, if you don't know how to get an edge that you can shave your arm with, read the section on sharpening now (see page 103).

Carving Letters

Now, to have at it. Clamp the piece of wood down to your workbench—protecting the work face with a pad between it and the clamp jaw—and pick up your knife. In this exercise, we will incise the letters with a V-cut at least 1/4 inch deep. The deeper the cut, the bolder the shadow line in the finished letter. (Don't be weak-kneed about depth in any carving; it's what you want.) With the knife, make a cut down the center and at the ends of every letter (Figure 9a). Known as a "stop-cut," it does just that—it stops the wood from splitting away. (Someone once told me it is the single most important cut he had learned in carving.) Now, if all you own is the knife, make a sloped cut with it to remove the wood from each side of the line (Figure 9b). Don't try to

10 • **Block letters carved with a knife, using a paring motion.**

take it all out at once; leave at least 1/32 inch near the outside edge for final cleanup. You will have to cut down the centerline repeatedly as you go. The ends of the letters may be cut vertically or on the same slope as the sides (Figure 9c). This is the old "heart and initials on the apple tree" carving, but nice work has been done this way.

If you are using a chisel as well as a knife, make a series of cuts into the centerline of each letter—after making stop-cuts with your knife—leaving "cleanup" wood at the edge, as before. Using a knife, a chisel, or a skew chisel, make the final cuts with a paring motion along the length of the line (Figures 9d and 10). The skew chisel is sometimes held like a pencil, and

11 • Two methods of holding the carving tool.

19

drawn toward you. Pare away only as much thickness as you can control.

Thus far, we have been talking only about letters that have rectangular-ended strokes. Any letters that look like those in Figure 5 and have a V-incised cross section can be carved with a knife, a skew chisel, or a similar flat-sided tool. When you progress from this style of letter to those with rounded ends, you'll need tools with curved blades to do a proper job.

For the letters shown in Figure 6, the V cross section no longer works well. Veiners and U-gouges are used to carve the curved ends, and the curve is carried right down to form the cross section of the incised letter. Having several U-gouges of different sizes makes this type of letter easier to carve. It's a more attractive and graceful style of lettering and one that you'll want to experiment with as you acquire more tools. The one lettering style you'll want to avoid like shoal water is that with rounded ends to the strokes and no serifs. This is the kind of lettering you could easily do with an electric router, and I can think of no reason to make any hand carving look like that.

If you wish to speed up the work, you can make all the vertical stop-cuts in all the letters first, then the horizontal ones, followed by the curves. Later on, when you are experienced, you will find yourself following a schedule of similar cuts right across the board. It saves the frequent picking up and putting down of tools and the body moves that go with them. If you're a beginner—or are trying out a new style of lettering—you'll probably find it much more enjoyable to complete one letter before starting the next. There are pleasures even in small accomplishments.

The Ends, and Finishing

Assuming now that your lettering is carved, all that is left are the decorative feather ends (Figures 12, 13, and 14). The first step is to drill a body hole for the size of roundhead screw that you plan to use for attachment. Next, cut the outside shape of the design, using either the knife or a fret saw, scroll saw, or bandsaw. Now make stop-cuts along each line, and then pare the horizontal bevels with the knife or the chisel. If you used the chisel on the letters, you held it flat, face down, to get a straight line cut; on these curving surfaces, turn it over, bevel-side down, to get a sweeping curve. Leave enough of a "land" around the screw hole to support the screw head. To make the lines of the feather stand out more, bevel the vertical edges in toward the back, as shown in Figure 14.

If you are right-handed, push the tool with your right hand, cupping the handle in your right palm; this hand also does most of the steering. The fingers of your left hand hold the tool near its cutting end, and perform the duplicate operation of fine steering and holding back the tool to prevent it

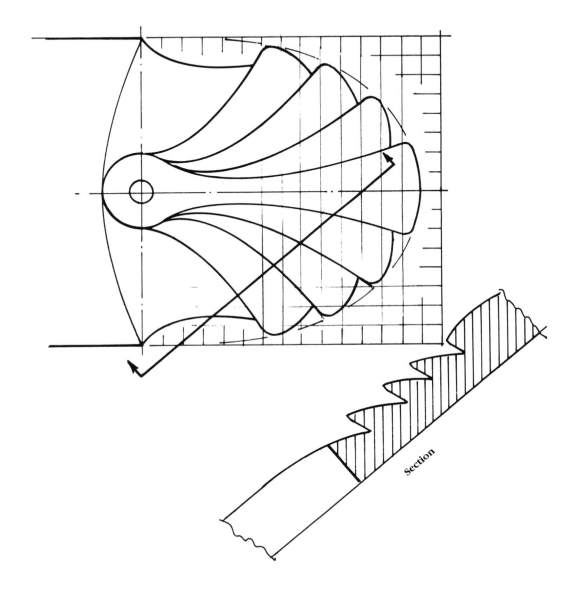

Section

12 • A design for a simple feather at the ends of a nameboard.

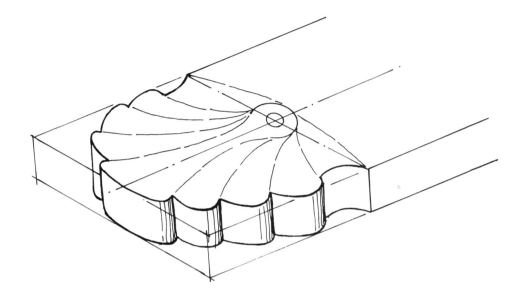

13 • Feather end outline cut to shape.

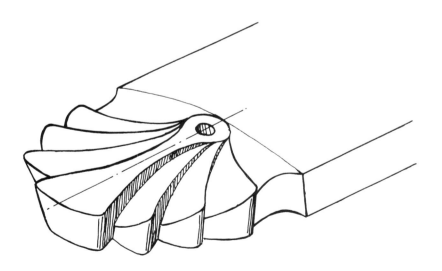

14 • Feather end, with bevels carved.

15 • **A slightly more elaborate feather end.**

from overcutting. If you have some unaccustomed muscle ache at the end of the day, that's what did it—pushing with one hand while holding back with the other. There really are no hard-and-fast rules for where your hands grip the tool, so find the position that is most comfortable for you. (See Figure 11.) Final cleanup cuts are done more with fingertip control rather than with your full hand.

A carving tool really doesn't care if you are right-handed or left-handed. In fact, carving a curved line or surface is like beating upwind: It can't be done all on one tack. Mounting the work on a corner of the bench will permit more movement of your body in relation to the board, but you will still find times when it's necessary to shift the tool to the other hand—so learn to use both hands. It's not all that difficult.

Except for roughing out, all carving should be done as much as possible with long, easy cuts, so that the finished job looks carved, not picked at. If you are using a V-gouge, the carving should be a series of progressively deeper cuts. Be careful to stop in time at the end of each stroke. The idea is to make many small, shallow cuts, rather than to hack out a mass of large splinters!

The cardinal rule of carving wood is to cut with the grain, and yet it is forgotten at times in the enjoyment of carving. And you can't always cut with the grain; probably about half of your work will be across it. Try to make sure that the grain runs *into* the area to be cut, not out of it; then, if a split starts, it will run into the wood that is to be removed. Of course, this is not always possible to do. If you are using a V-gouge and the grain runs diagonally to the cut, one lip of the gouge will be cutting with the grain, and one against it. The answer here is to make fine cuts, use sharp tools, and—once the initial cut has been made—to remove material with the edge that is cutting with the grain. If you get in a position where you are not sure which way to cut (and you won't be alone if you do), think of the grain lines as level lines in a landscape and the carving tool as a ski sliding always downhill, the hill being the wood you want to keep.

If the board is to be finished bright and you haven't already stained it, do so now. Carry through whatever finishing schedule you are using, right to the last coat of varnish, then go back to the letters and the ends and paint them. This way, if you overrun the letter outlines, you can wipe off the surface with a cloth just barely dampened with turps or paint thinner. A good-looking board can be painted black all over, with letters and ends yellow or gold-leafed. Don't paint carved letters black; as I've said before, the shadow lines are what bring out the carving, and shadows show up very poorly on black.

Now that the board is done, look at it very critically to see what you would do differently next time. The details that will be the most obvious to you are where the chisel slipped, or where you didn't cut a curve just right. Put the board away for a couple of months (the paint really has to harden, doesn't it?), and then bring it out again. By this time, you will have forgotten those places where you made the little goofs, and you'll see the board as others see it. Looks pretty good, doesn't it? And so you say, "If I can do that, I can carve a stern eagle." So you can, but how about another cut or two along the practice route before trying?

4 • Sternboards

If you're ready to take a chance with a bigger piece of wood, let's consider a transom nameboard, or sternboard. Again, design is most important. Do a lot of doodling and sketching. The primary controls are, of course, the shape and size of the transom, and the goal is to make a sternboard that fits. You don't want a billboard, but neither do you want something that looks too small. One board for the name and another for the port of call is a good arrangement. (This helps if you goof; then only part of the work goes into the stove.)

Large powerboat transoms seem to carry much larger lettering in proportion to their size than do sailboat sterns. Now, you can say that this is due to the larger ego of the powerboat owners, or to the shy, retiring nature of the sailboat owners; or maybe it's because the powerboats go by so fast that you have to be able to read the name quickly. Of course, a large sternboard is a benefit to the sailor who wants to know whom he's swearing at when a passing powerboat wake nearly swamps him in a narrow thoroughfare. Conversely, it gives him a chance to mentally thank by name the true powerboat sailor who slows down for him.

The curves should be agreeable with the shape of the transom (Figure 16). If there is a lot of rake to the transom, a board viewed from astern will be foreshortened in height, and so letters on a curving board will appear to be somewhat less curved, and horizontal curves will be foreshortened and flattened.

A gentle or graceful name should appear on that kind of board; likewise, a strong name should be reflected in strong design and lettering.

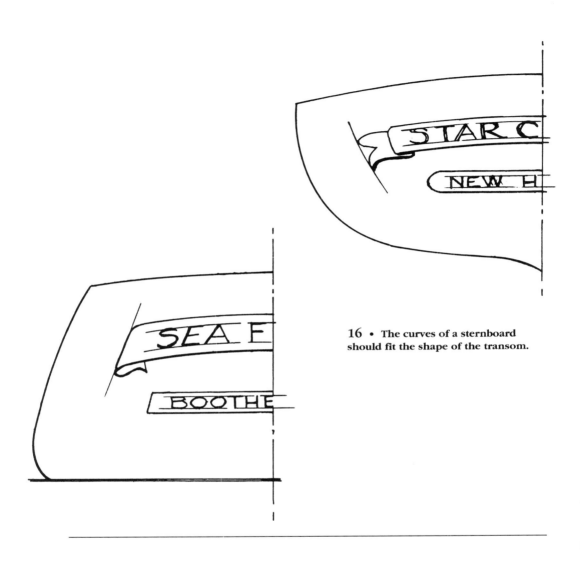

16 • **The curves of a sternboard should fit the shape of the transom.**

There are two types of carving, one of which we've already tried—carving in, which is termed "incised." When the carved part stands out, it's "in relief"—bas-relief, if it's low. (The "bas" in bas-relief is pronounced as a Mainer says "Bar Harbor", or as a sheep says "baa.") High relief stands out more and so has more shape. It's also more prone to breakage and requires thicker wood to begin with—two of the reasons why we see more incised work on boats today.

Remember that you are working in wood, so don't make fragile units or intricate carvings that will break off. No water-holding hollows in the carving, either—everything should slope so that drainage is easy.

Banners or wide ribbons seem to lend themselves best to sternboards and are simple and quite effective (see Chapter 5). The middle is usually kept smooth, and the ends are waved, curled, or tapered (Figure 21). Most of the curling is an illusion fostered by the outline shape of the board and emphasized by enough surface carving to create shadows. Soft and gentle surface curves and slowly rounded edges lose their effectiveness, because they don't have strong shadows.

Board ends can be finished off with the ever-popular stylized dolphins (see Chapter 6) or other fish, or you can carve ornaments—stars, or other traditional motifs—or something original to fit the name. Our boat's name, *Urchin,* came about because she was sort of raggedy when we got her; the sea urchins on her sternboard relate the name to the ocean (Figure 17). You have a chance to let your imagination run wild on designs, but work toward the conservative end of the scale—remember that it's a boat, not a circus wagon, that you're embellishing.

If you are doing something like the dolphin shown in Figure 30, you can saw out the fish shapes on a bandsaw and epoxy-glue them to the upper surface of the board ends. This gives you material for high-relief carving,

17 • **Decorations on nameboards work best when they relate to the name of the boat.**

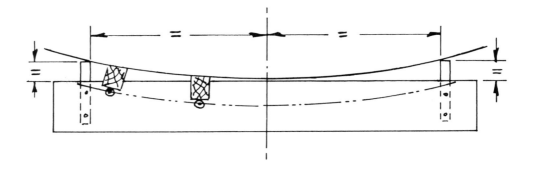

18 • Spiling off the curve of a transom.

whereas the letters are incised. By using just the board thickness alone, an effective job can be done in low relief. Cut a deep-V outline at the intersection of the fish and the board, and model the fish. Of course, if your boat is named *Pequod*, you'll want to change to whales and paint them white. Stars (see pages 34–35 and Figures 26–29) are more satisfactory if incised. Actually, a star in relief looks nicer (see Figure 42), but the points where the grain crosses are very fragile.

A rope border (see Chapter 7) is another old favorite. Again, this can be done in low relief (the same height as the board surface), or it can be added on and then carved. The rope ends may be a Flemish coil, a fancy knot, or whatever your imagination dictates. Designed and carved nicely, rope makes a good-looking border, but unless you don't mind repetitive work, you're going to wish by the time you're halfway through the job that you'd never started. But bear with it—you can't go sailing yet, anyway.

What else can you do? Carve birds in the board ends if your boat is named after a bird; or carve one separately (see Chapter 10) and mount it between the name and the port of call. I don't know what you can do if your boat has one of those hybrid names made up of the first two letters of several persons' names. You named her; you figure it out.

Fitting the Board to the Transom

You should give some thought to how the board is to be fastened to the transom. The first thing that comes to mind is to use through-planking screws, with the heads inside the transom. However, this can pose problems in a wooden boat with a decked-over stern: One, it may be difficult to locate the screws so that they hit neither seams nor frames; two, it may be hard getting to

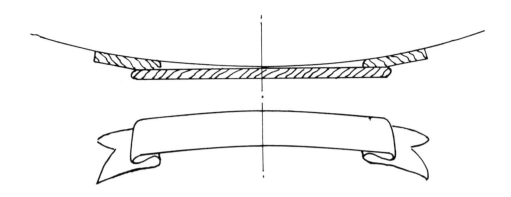

19 • Using sloped end pads on a curved transom.

the inside of the transom to turn the screw. On a fiberglass boat, it might not be so difficult. The greatest objection I have to this is putting through-holes in any planking. A boat as old as ours has enough leaks without our drilling holes in her—even if they are above the waterline.

Screws put in from the face of the board are easier to get at, and need not penetrate through the transom. Flatheads can be sunk and plugged, which looks well, but they are difficult to remove—and removing the sternboard is something that you will be doing, to repaint the transom or to take the board home in winter to restore the varnish. Roundheads that show can sometimes be worked into the design, as on the feather ends of the sample nameboard; this method is by far the easiest and most practical.

The board can be drawn up tight to the transom, and, if this is to be done, it's a good idea to cover the whole back of the board with bedding compound before installing it. Without the compound, there is a good chance of water getting in between and starting rot. I prefer to use rubber or neoprene washers (from a plumbing supply house) between the transom and the board. This keeps the board about 1/8 inch away from the transom and permits drainage and ventilation; it also allows for minor discrepancies in fitting.

Most transoms have an athwartship curve that the sternboard must follow. If the curve is very slight, the board can be sprung to the transom with the fastenings. To aid a spring fit, make vertical saw cuts on the back of the board (about 1/2 inch apart and not quite half the board's thickness in depth), across the middle three-quarters of its length. If you follow this procedure, squeeze some flexible caulking into the saw kerfs before bending, to seal out moisture. On excessively curved transoms, the board will have to be bent to fit. The actual curve can be taken off by spiling.

One fairly easy way to spile off a curve is shown in Figure 18. Draw a centerline down the transom. Then, find a light board that is somewhat longer than the proposed sternboard. Draw a centerline across it, and nail equal-length spacers at each end, equidistant from the centerline. The spacers must project far enough to include the transom curve. Hold the board against the transom with the centerlines in line, and, with a pencil held against a block that slides along the face of the transom, draw a line on the board. This will be easier if you nail the pencil to the block with staples. Back in the workshop, remove the end spacers and place another board alongside the first. By turning the pencil and block around and following the first line, a second line can be drawn on the new board. This is the transom curve.

The bending should be done after rough-sawing the shape of the board. You won't need a steam box; just wrap the board in rags and pour hot water over it. Keep it hot-wet for a while, then clamp it to a form with the right curve

20 • The boat's name can give you ideas for end decorations. For example, *Fiddlers' Green*'s sternboard has curling fiddlehead ends. Saint Malo is a French port, so fleurs-de-lis were used on the port-of-hail board. "Båten" means "The Boat" in Norwegian, so a Scandinavian design was used on the ends of *Båten*'s nameboard (above). Since *Old Baldy* has an American bald eagle for a figurehead (see Figure 78), her sternboard ends (below) are simply decorated with stars. Below left is *Whitehawk*'s handsome stern, with carvings by Peter Libbey.

and leave it to dry. I'd leave the piece on the form under clamps for at least two days; be sure to put pads between the clamps and the wood so you won't end up with some lovely dents to sand out.

Of course, you can cheat and avoid the whole bending bit if you design the board with sloped end pads, as in Figure 19—but, frankly, the results aren't exactly appealing. A board with end pads looks good on a flat surface, though.

On this job, I hope you'll do more carving and increase your tool range. If you're using a wood that is harder than pine, a mallet will save you much labor. A woodcarver's mallet (see Figure 88 in Chapter 13, "Tools and Sharpening") looks something like an old-fashioned potato masher. It has the advantage of always having its face in line with the tool end, and it is used with taps, not hammer blows.

5 · Banner or Ribbon Ends

Banners—or ribbons, as they are called in old English carving books—are reasonably easy to carve and look very good for the effort expended. But the carver must take the time to analyze the curves and surfaces involved. The wood cannot be thinned down to the thickness of an actual ribbon, but should appear as if it were.

Make a drawing of the banner end on tracing paper (Figure 22), transfer it to both ends of the work piece, and saw away the waste. I find that it helps to draw a line on the vertical edges to indicate roughly how the end is to be folded and waved, and to provide a guide for cutting depths. (Our example was carved from 3/4-inch pine and was thinned down to about 3/8 inch in the center of the return fold.) With the board clamped to the workbench, "set in" (that is, outline and block out, as described on page 42) the shapes, and cut out the center groove. Remember that the outline of the piece is what dictates the surface you are carving, except that you are foreshortening the curves in depth. If you have one, use a sharp, inside-ground gouge, and cut across the grain. Make the top edge of this surface a little flatter than the lower, as the distance across the top appears to be greater. In other words, think of this as a ribbon, and curve it accordingly. Round the edges of the top surfaces as they curl down, and undercut the curl slightly (Figure 23).

Take a minute away from the carving now to think about undercutting. All this means is to cut away, to some extent, the underside of whatever element you are carving. To repeat what's been said before, light and shadow are what define shape and depth to the eye, and by increasing a shadow prop-

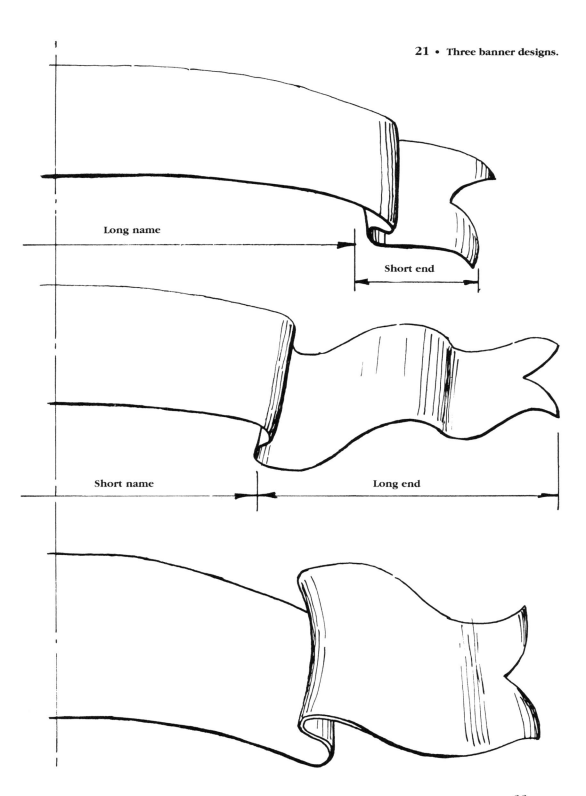

Long name

Short end

Short name

Long end

erly, you can fool the eye into believing something is much rounder than it really is.

Looking at Figure 24a, which might be a cross section of a vine stem, you can see that if you round just the top surface and then come down straight to the background, the element will only look round from straight on. Now, if you undercut the back of the stem, as in Figure 24b, you can create a shadow that makes it harder for the eye to see what is there. The brain interprets this to mean that what it can't see on the back must be like what's on the front—that is, round. Magic, isn't it? If you undercut even more, as in Figure 24c, the shadow deepens, and the brain says the stem is even rounder. In marine carving, you don't want to undercut anything to the point of fragility, but for a purely decorative panel for your house, extreme undercutting can be an interesting thing to play with.

The easiest way to carve the reverse curves at the bottom of the ribbon is first to cut across them, parallel with the lower edge, with a U-gouge. Make one curve for the top curl and one for the bottom curl. Redraw the curl line, and round the vertical outside curves (Figure 25).

Now for the tricky part. Consider the bottom edge of the ribbon, inboard of the curl. It's a vertical surface (with the board clamped to the bench). Following it along outboard, carve it vertically until you come to where it rolls back. Carve the horizontal surface in to meet it. Repeat on the lower curl. (It's harder to describe than to do.) Undercut the verticals slightly, except for a narrow strip that indicates the ribbon thickness. Now, put some waves in the ribbon end. Because the ribbon end divides into two separate pieces, you can carve the wave differently in each to give it more life. (See Figure 26.)

If the ribbon shapes bother or puzzle you, cut a piece of heavy cloth to the width of your ribbon and drape it over some wood scraps, books, or what-have-you and use it for a model. It helps.

You can decorate each banner end with a star (see Figure 27 and the next section). Then, to finish up, bevel back the top and bottom edges of the board, the top to a greater degree. Stand the board up and view it from slightly above, checking to see that it looks the way you wish it to. Painting the edges of the board black also helps produce the illusion of thinness.

The Star

The star is a simple, straight-lined, incised carving that is used traditionally on ribbon ends. On a light piece of cardboard, draw a circle the size of the star's outside diameter. Divide the circumference into five equal parts, and connect the points. Cut out the star, and you have a pattern that will conform to the waves in the board. After drawing around the pattern, draw lines connecting

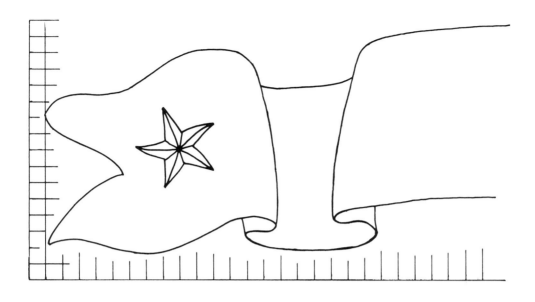

22 • A banner-end design.

each point with the opposite indent (Figure 27). These are the lines, from the center out, on which to make your stop-cuts.

To digress a little: The star is frequently used in carving, and I finally got tired of laying out a new one for each job because the old pattern was the wrong size or had been swept up with the chips. Laziness is the mother of invention, and so some inspired thought produced the handy little gidget shown in Figure 29. You can make one from a 6-inch square of .030-inch clear, flexible plastic. Put a small dent in the center. Then set your dividers at 1/2-inch, and scribe a circle of 1-inch diameter. Using the same center, scribe concentric circles of the following diameters: 1-1/2 inch; 2, 3, 4, and 5 inches. With a protractor, carefully lay out radii 72 degrees apart. With the sharp point of your dividers, carefully scribe lines from those points to the center. At the center and at each intersection, drill a small hole just large enough to get the point of a pencil through. Connect the proper points on the large circle with scribed lines for a star, and if you want to, do the same on one of the smaller circles. (This is not really necessary, but it does help to eliminate confusion.) The next time you want a star, put the template over the area on the carving or drawing where you want it, pick the size circle that looks right, and poke your pencil point through the center hole and the five holes on the circle. Remove the gidget, put it away for next time, connect all the dots, and go to it.

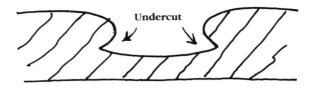

23 • **Cross section of an undercut curl in a banner.**

24 • **Three steps of undercutting a vine stem. The blackened areas of the cross sections show increased shadowing from undercutting.**

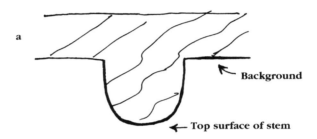

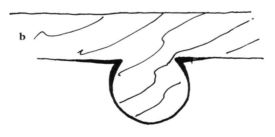

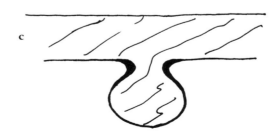

25 • Carving the reverse curves at the bottom of a banner.

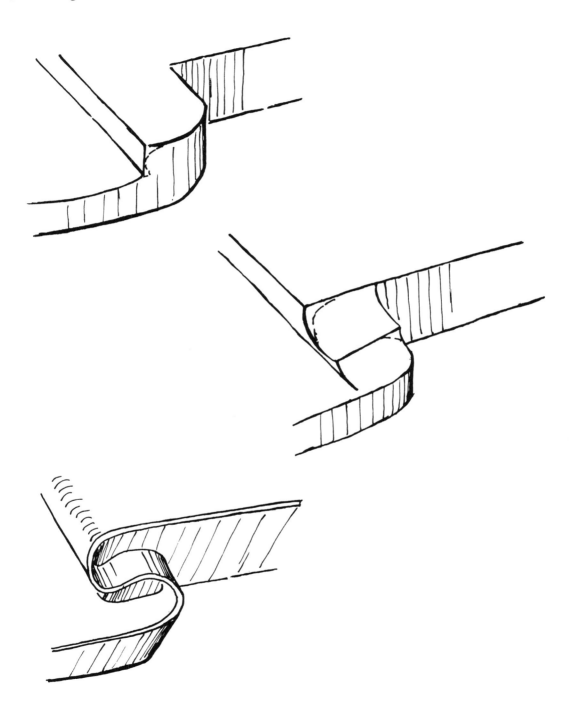

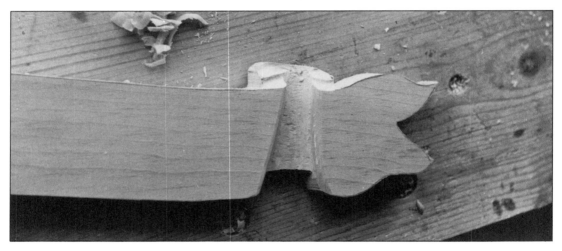

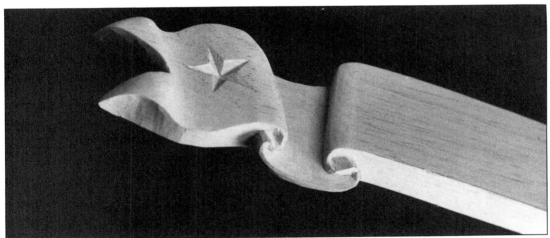

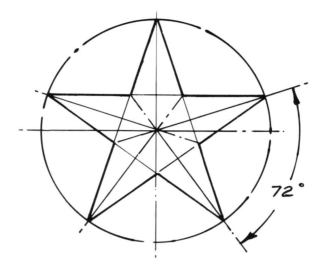

72°

27 • **The configuration of a star.**

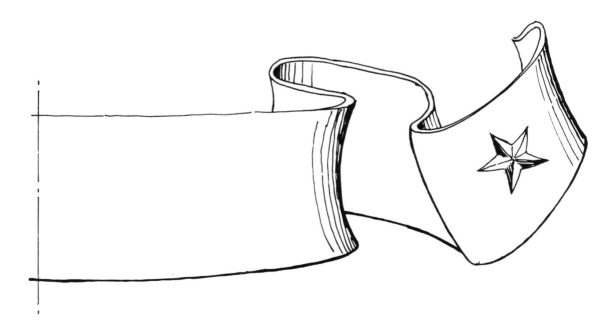

28 • **An incised star decorates a "curling" banner end.**

40

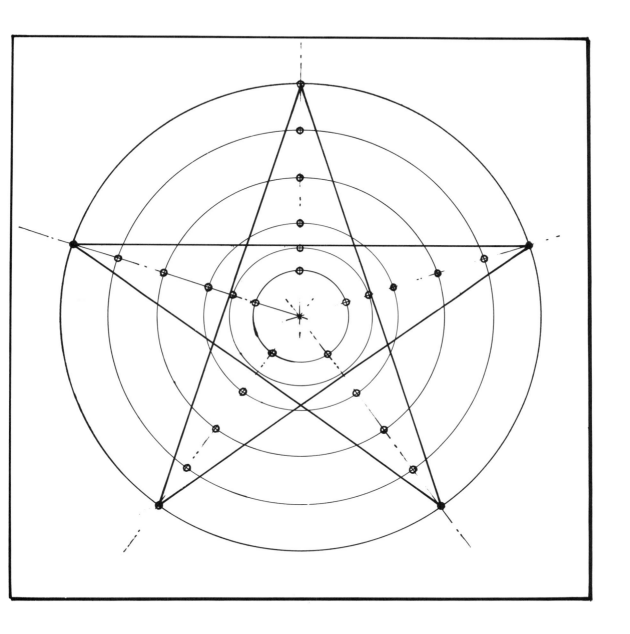

29 • Design for a star template, to be made of clear plastic.

6 • Dolphins

Let's try carving a dolphin as an example of a different type of board end, although almost everything said in this section applies equally well to carving a bird, a whale, or a horseshoe crab.

No one says that you have to use my dolphin drawing (Figure 30); it's just here to illustrate the techniques. First of all, in all the nautical miles I've covered, I've never seen a fish like this. However, as I stated, marine carving is usually traditional, and this drawing approaches the traditional dolphin design. Look up the drawings of fish that decorate old charts, or look at photos of old carvings; then design your own, if you wish, or use this one.

The simplest approach to the carving is just to cut grooves everywhere there is a line. For this you need about a 1/16-inch or 2mm veiner gouge (a gouge that cuts a deep, narrow U—see Figure 86). In this case, the effect of roundness is achieved by the way the dolphin is drawn. Notice, for instance, that the scales are not drawn in a random pattern, but in a way that leads the eye to believe there is a roundness to the body.

You could, instead, make the outline cuts deeper, and then emphasize the shape by low-relief carving.

After tracing the design (at the desired size) on both ends of the board, making sure that one dolphin looks to port and one to starboard, saw out the waste. Setting in is next. To "set in" the lines means to outline the design with vertical cuts. This is done for two reasons: one, to carry the design we drew on the surface down to the depth it will be "in the round"; and two, to serve as stop-cuts. The wood is then cut down around the design to the different levels of ground. (This has been explained more completely in Chapter 9, "Trail-boards," on page 67, because the oak leaf design has a more involved setting-in process.) I used a knife, a 1/4-inch-wide chisel, a 1/2-inch gouge (inside-ground), and a mallet. When cutting down around the design, don't try to cut the whole depth at once—take it in steps. Also, cut a little outside of the lines so that you have something left for the finish cuts. The lowest flat plane that forms the background for a relief carving—in this case, the area surrounded by the head and the body—is known as the "ground," and cutting and level-ing it is part of the setting-in operation. Grounds can be cut as smoothly as possible, or tool marks from a nearly flat gouge may be left (as long as they are not so pronounced that they detract from the design). In this carving, the ground was about 5/16 inch below the board face. Figure 31 shows the work at this stage.

Make stop-cuts around the "hair," fins, and eye, then start lowering and rounding the shapes. At this stage, I used 1/8-inch and 3/8-inch skews, 1/8-inch and 1/4-inch gouges, and a 1/8-inch bent skew. This is a good time to add

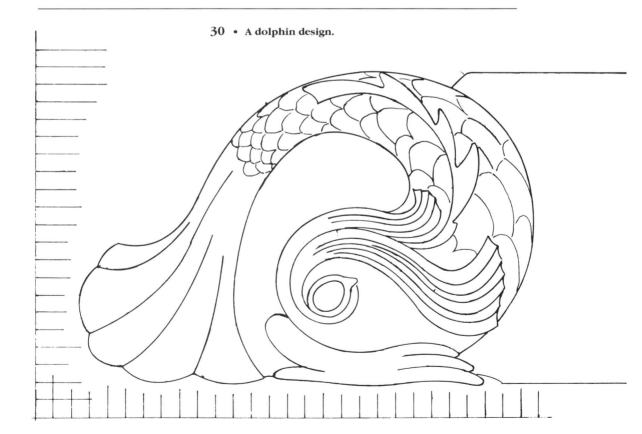

30 • A dolphin design.

31 • Dolphin cut down to the ground.

32 • A dolphin nameboard end.

some tools to your collection; the skews are handy tools for getting into corners. Unlike the carpenter's chisel or firmer, which is beveled on one side only, carvers' firmers are ground equally on both sides. In addition, the skew firmer is ground at an angle to the tool axis; this way, it can get into corners. For tighter corners with high sides, there are "bent" tools, which are beveled on the top edge. A right and a left bent skew should be early additions to your tool drawer. (See Chapter 13, "Tools and Sharpening.")

With the whole design blocked in and rounded out, start with the highest details—in this case, the "hair," or "mane." The swirls were cut with the 1/8-inch veiner, as was most of the detailing. Use the 1/4-inch gouge for wider and shallower valleys. The scales could be made as overlapping plates, but I made this carving in pine, in a rather small size (4-1/2-inch board width), so that method would have been pretty tricky. Instead, I just outlined all the scales with the 1/8-inch veiner to produce strong shadow lines (Figure 32); this way, I also avoided making fragile edges.

Rounding to the back of the board need be done at the top and ends only if this nameboard is to be mounted on a small boat, and hence viewed from above. And that's another thing about designing for carving: The viewing angle is important, particularly for surfaces that you wish to appear thin or fragile. Figure 33, which shows a profile view of a transom with sections at the top and bottom board edges, illustrates this.

Most "how-to's" on carving tell you never to use sandpaper. I'll go along with this for some carvings, but not all. I just don't believe it should be regarded as a sacrilege. If you are an experienced Swiss carver who makes every cut clean, sure, and positive, then you don't need to smooth anything. Sandpapering a massive carving in oak can only detract from it. But for us unskilled workers in softwoods who are trying to make a decoration that we'll enjoy looking at, I think sandpaper can help in places. Just remember not to spoil what you have worked hard to get. Sharp, strong edges should not be rounded and lost, and tool marks that add to the design should not be sanded out. If you find that you can't round the eyeball of the dolphin smoothly with a tool, finish it off by filing or sanding. Sandpaper glued to flexible wood strips can be used as curved files, which you can conform to the shape you want. Emery boards (for fingernails) work well, as you can cut them to any width and shape you need in order to get into awkward places. A word of caution about abrasive papers: Try not to use any until you are all through with carving. They slough off minute particles that can stay embedded in the wood and will quickly take the edge off a sharp tool. For finish work you can buy small files, both curved and straight, in many different shapes. These are known as riffler files. Smooth the wood as you wish, but please don't hold a sheet of sandpaper in your hand and rub over the whole design.

When you are satisfied with your carving, give it a coat of primer on the back as well as on the front if it is to be painted or gold-leafed. I like white-pigmented shellac for this job if the carving is to be used inside, as it dries quickly and stiffens the wood fibers. For outside work, a good marine primer-sealer should be used. With the whole carving flat white, it's easy to spot places that need more cleanup. Look at the carving from all angles, and sharpen up any intersections of surfaces that are fuzzy.

So there you are with a nice-looking board end. When doing a pair like this—one design the mirror image of the other—it is smart to work on both ends, one step at a time, rather than completing first one end and then the other. This way, there is more chance that the finished ends will look alike.

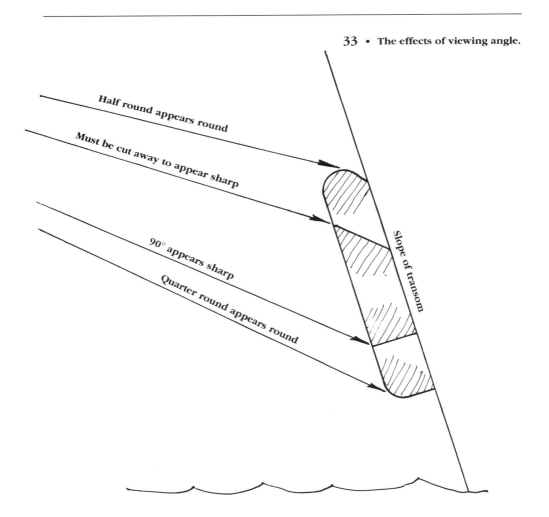

33 • The effects of viewing angle.

46

7 • Rope Borders

A rope border is most effective if it is higher than the board it surrounds, but you can carve it using just the board thickness if you wish. In the latter case, make a heavy V-cut first, defining the edge of the rope where it meets the face of the board. The next step is to round the rope on the front and top edges and bevel toward the back of the board (see Figure 34).

To make a raised rope border, either cut down the face of the board inside the rope edge (a long job!), or glue on the face edge a strip that is the width of the rope diameter and a little more than half the rope diameter in height (see Figure 35). If you curve around the ends, it is smart to make that curve with separate pieces of wood to keep the grain running as nearly as possible with the rope axis. For assembly, use waterproof glue and small wire brads (don't drive them in all the way). When the glue is hard, pull the nails; left in, they make carving difficult, and what they do to a cutting edge will keep you busy at the sharpening stone for quite a spell.

Let's assume that, however you are making it, the rope border is now rounded and ready for the rest of the carving. To lay out the strands, run a centerline along the front face of the rope axis, and mark off spaces that are roughly equal to the rope diameter (Figure 36). Cut a piece of light, flexible cardboard at an angle to its base of slightly greater than 30 degrees. Roll this template over a dowel to give it a curve, and, with the base edge down in the groove, draw the strand separations. Now make stop-cuts on each of these lines and cut in to a V, or use a V-parting tool. Next, round each strand. Keep in mind that the strands are true rounds, and if it makes it easier for you, draw a centerline on each to indicate the highest part. That is, although we carved

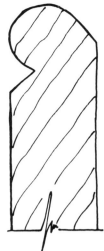 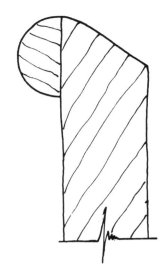

34 • A rope border level with the board face.   35 • A rope border above the board face.

the overall rope shape with a horizontal axis, switch your mind around so that you think of each strand as a round with a diagonal axis. The need for this will become very apparent once you start carving the strands. If you keep a short piece of rope in front of you while you are working, there will be no problem. The intersection of the strands and the V-cut of the board should appear as in Figure 37, to emphasize the roundness of the strands. Figure 37 shows the four steps, from right to left: marking, stop-cuts, V-cuts, and rounding. Clean up the finished work with sandpaper sticks or riffler files.

For a rope border on the periphery of a transom, cut and fit together pieces of sized stock all around the transom, tacking them in place with fine-wire nails and keeping the grain running as nearly as possible with the rope axis. Number each piece so that they can be reassembled in the same order. Removed from the boat, they can now be carved in the shop. When carving at a

36 • Laying out the proportions of a rope border.

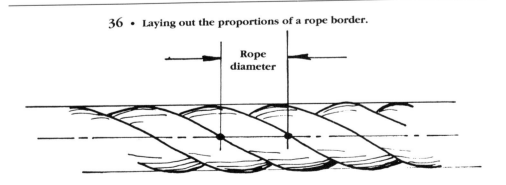

Rope diameter

48

joint, match the two pieces together to maintain continuity between the strands. This can be done by lightly gluing the pieces to paper, which in turn is glued to a board. If the transom is curved, so must the backing board be, or the joints won't fit properly. After being carved, the rope can be split off the backing piece, and all the paper can be removed from the carving. Double-surfaced, pressure-sensitive tape works well instead of paper and glue, and is easier to remove.

If you are in doubt about achieving the right shape and curve to your backing board, just carve the strands, except at the joints. Permanently assemble and fix the border to the transom, and then carve the joint areas. This method will result in the smoothest appearance—that is, unless you're attempting the job while the boat is afloat and you're in a dinghy. Rope work mounted this way should portray just half the rope diameter.

Rope carving is tedious; but done nicely, the finished job, all shiny with gold leaf (an example is shown on page 30), is handsome and well worth the effort. About halfway through, you'll begin to wish you could just nail on some real rope, but stick with it—real rope doesn't take on a good paint job, anyway.

Good luck!

37 • The four steps in carving a rope border (from right to left): marking, stop-cuts, V-cuts, and rounding.

8 • Billetheads and Fiddleheads

One of the most effective bits of decoration on a boat is the one up forward that points the way, whether it's a figurehead dipping up and down with the swells or just a simplified scroll called a billethead or fiddlehead. The two names define the type of the scroll: A billethead rolls down, whereas a fiddlehead, as on a violin, rolls up.

The first requirement for this type of decoration is a stemhead projecting out under the bowsprit (see Figure 38). If your boat doesn't have a bowsprit, it shouldn't have a forward-projecting stemhead. This type of head was originally designed as a lashing point for the bowsprit, and without one the addition of a projecting head looks fake. A long, slim head should carry a light figure or billethead. The point is to emphasize your boat's graceful lines, not to blunt or distort them.

Some billetheads are carved from the stemhead itself, but most are added on. The carving can be screwed or bolted on in the form of a rabbeted joint, which permits removal for repair or replacement in case of damage. It's also easier to carve a small piece that can be moved around on your workbench than to manhandle a whole stemhead.

On a boat with trailboards, the billethead design will be the forward termination of the trailboard design. The trailboard rails, top and bottom, run into and end in a swirl at the billet. Without trailboards, the billethead is just a nice way to end the stem; it certainly adds character and individuality to your craft.

Now that you are familiar enough with carving tools so that your palms don't get sweaty at the thought of cutting into that blank piece of wood, it's time to try something that you haven't tackled before: carving in the round. A billethead really has two sides and an edge or face, but it will be a better carving if you think of the sides as part of the face. That is, roll some of the side carving around the corners to make the design "in the round." The example shown in Figure 39 has a minimum of this, but enough to introduce you to the thinking. So let's get on with it.

Because the billethead is to be carved on all sides, the problem of holding it is a little more complex than it was for a flat board. The easiest answer is to make up the block, and, having cut the rabbeted joint where the carving is to attach to the stem, make another block to fit the rabbet—sort of a dummy stem that can be held in the vise or clamped to the workbench (Figure 40).

Having transferred the design to the block, on both sides, set in the outline cuts and cut down to the ground on the after end of the design. Next, drill holes for a couple of screws, one on each side in staggered positions, and fasten the two blocks together. Now, using a bandsaw, cut the outside shape.

Notice in Figure 39, sectional view, that the two round bands come in toward the center as they go forward, but that the center round that carries the star is the full thickness of the piece. Leave this thickness until all other carving is done (Figure 41); it helps support the ends when the piece is clamped on its side on the bench. The star is done last, in relief (the circle is hollowed in around it).

Follow this progression in making the billethead:

*Start with a piece of wood twice the length of the billethead. This will include both the billethead and the holding piece.
*Trace the design on both sides.
*Cut the block in two on the sloped after line of the billethead.
*Cut the rabbet joint.
*Set in lines and cut down to the ground at the after end of the billethead.
*Drill and screw the billethead to waste stock.

38 • The stemhead of a Friendship sloop model.

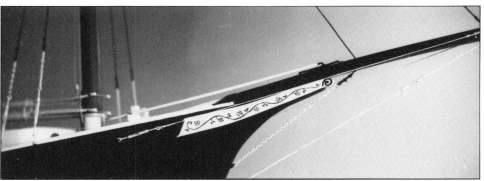

39 • A design for a billethead.

52

40 (above) • **The billethead with a dummy stem to hold it while you carve.**
41 (below) • **The billethead partially roughed out.**

*Bandsaw the shape.

*Set in lines around the inner circle, and cut the outer circle and bands to depth on both sides.

*Set in and cut the leaves and stems to depth.

*Rough-shape the leaves, stems, and outside rounds.

*Cut down the center of the outside face (front edge) to depth, and finish shaping the rounds.

*Draw the centerline and curving "scales" around the face of the billethead (see Figure 42).

*Carve the scales.

*Finish carving all over.

*Set in the edges of the star.

*Cut down the background around the star.

*Make stop-cuts on the star.

*Slope down from its center to the points.

*Bevel the point sides.

*Clean up all over the billethead.

42 • **The various surfaces of the billethead.**

I hesitate to tell anyone what textures to end up with on their own carving; it's so often a matter of personal choice. What I did on this billethead seemed to fit the design for me, but you do it the way you want to. I was going to finish off the outside rounds with a rope border, but as the carving progressed, it became apparent that in a small size this would appear too fussy, so I went to the other extreme and smoothed them round with sandpaper. The next circle was carved in with a shallow bent gouge, making the cuts from the outside toward the center. This produced very subtle ridges and scallops, which I left, feeling that the tool marks were attractive. The face of the inner circle was dished in to the center, and was carved smoothly so that the intersections of the star edges would be sharp.

Again, I want to emphasize that carvings are personal things, and in most cases the drawing or pattern that you use should not be regarded as a must.

What sometimes looks good on paper might not work in three dimensions. This is your work, and if you think the design can be improved while you're carving, go ahead and do it your way. Just temper your changes with the thought that, although you can easily cut more off, it's a little more difficult to put the wood back later if you don't like the change. In this same vein, if you break off a small chip on a leaf or other free-flowing design, it is usually pos-

43 • Old-fashioned style of billethead.

44 • **A billethead mounted as a wall decoration.**

sible to recarve to a slightly different line to save the piece. This, of course, won't work on controlled motifs such as a star or letters. Use great care, and take your time in situations where a slip would be costly. If you do slip badly, or if you find a pitch pocket or some other deformity in the wood right where you need a sharp edge (and this is, of course, where defects always show up), don't despair. You can drill out the bad spot and glue in a plug (see Figure 75), or you can cut it out and set in a graving piece, which is just a rectangular or other-shaped block to fit your cut-out recess. Make sure that your added piece fits well, and that the grain and its direction follow the surrounding wood.

Figures 43 and 44 show a design for a different style of billethead. Try something like this for pure enjoyment. All elements of the design should be cut deeply; give the leaves lots of shape so they are not just flat.

By this time, you should have a nice-looking billethead for a decoration, a bookend, or even for a boat that you can build to fasten to it.

9 • Trailboards

One wonders if the derivation of "trail" boards was simply "rail" boards, because that is the way they began. In the 18th century, ships had numerous rails running aft from the stemhead as supports. Two of these rails, or knees, with a filling board between them, remain today as trailboards.

An 18th-century trailboard, in effect, was made up of two long, slim knees, one above the other. These knees strengthened the stemhead in an athwartships direction, and the board that carried the decoration ran vertically between them. The rails formed a curved knee where they met and ran along the hull (Figure 45). Some vessels had a definite break in the board at this point (the stem rabbet line), with one piece of wood on the stem and another on the hull (Section b-b); others had the board all in one piece—or at least appearing so—with a curve instead of a break at the rabbet (Section b^1-b^1). The top and bottom rails were kept horizontal athwartships along the stemhead and where they met the hull shape, as illustrated in Sections a-a and c-c. This could be a tricky joinery job, but either way the design became complex. It looks simple in the profile drawing, but boats are seldom viewed from just this angle.

Traditional types of boats, such as the Friendship sloop and the Chesapeake Bay bugeye, have trailboard shapes and carvings that have become set for that type (see Figure 46). If you are decorating such a boat, it is wise to follow in the tradition, at least as far as the shape and type of ornamentation go. Friendship sloops have a simplified vine decoration, but no one says that the vine has to be kept simple. Some of the Chesapeake Bay vessels, such as

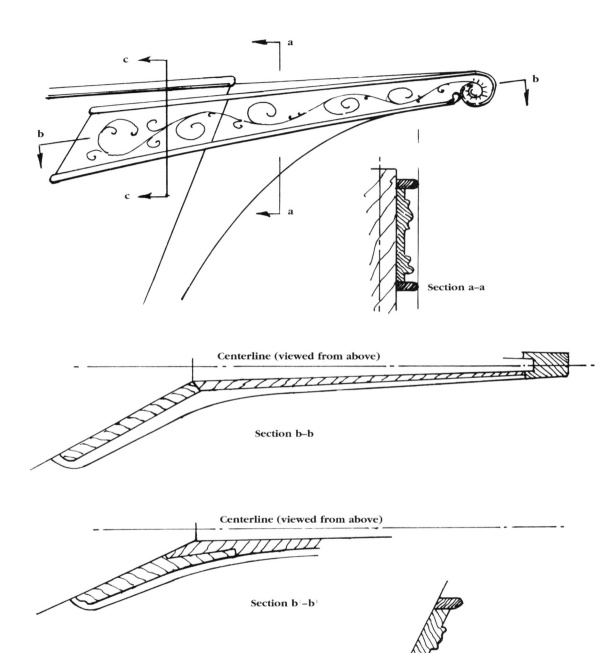

Section a–a

Centerline (viewed from above)

Section b–b

Centerline (viewed from above)

Section b'–b'

Section c–c

45 • Two different methods for making up a trailboard.

46 • *Sazerac* (above), an old Friendship sloop rebuilt by Bald Mountain Boat Works, has traditional bow decorations, an incised leaf scroll. Patriotic motifs were used on the trailboards of *Rebecca T. Ruark* (below), a Chesapeake Bay sloop built in 1886 by Moses Geoghegan.

bateaux and bugeyes, have very long, slim trailboards that carry all kinds of designs—a leaf scroll, frequently the vessel's name, and sometimes American shields or other motifs—so this type of boat offers great scope for your imagination.

Trailboards for a nontraditional type of boat can be designed to please the owner, but there are some rules to follow. The first is to keep all lines in harmony with the hull lines. The second is to remember that you are adding a decoration to the boat—so make it fit the boat. I've seen some boards that completely destroy a bow shape, or that are gaudy enough to make a seagull puke. The late L. Francis Herreshoff had the finest touch for good decorative design that I've ever seen, but why not? He believed hull design to be closer to sculpture than anything else.

Fore-and-aft lines follow and are directed by the lines of the bowsprit, sheer, and planking; vertical lines are directed by the stem. The idea is to have a trailboard that continues the hull lines with no sudden breaks or dips. The upper and lower rails of the board are the defining lines, and these roll into the billethead and become part of it. All fore-and-aft lines should taper as they run forward. The total effect should be that the decorative work appears to be part of the boat, not something stuck on to dress her up. Remember, she's a lady.

I would suggest, if you are building the complete board, that you first make a pattern by taping heavy paper to the bow and stem, making sure that it is pulled in to the rabbet, and then drawing the board and its rails. Remove the paper, carefully cut out the shape, and tape it back in place. This is a good way to observe how the board will look from different angles. Walk around, getting back a ways. Remember where the waterline is; you'll rarely observe the trailboards from lower than 3 feet above it (that's about eye height from a dinghy). If you are satisfied with the appearance, transfer the outside lines to the hull and stem. The next step is to make light pine patterns of the top and bottom rails with the correct bevels. For the rails to be kept horizontal in the athwartship plane, the part of the board lying on the hull will have to be made of pretty thick stuff so that it can be molded to fit the hull shape; and as I stated earlier, the board as well as the rails should be thickest at their after ends, tapering as they run forward. No one can tell you step by step how to construct the whole thing, but with these hints for guides, and good woodworking skills, you can do it.

The rails and board should be fastened together, and the unit should be held to the boat with screws. This way, when all is fitted, the complete unit can be removed for carving on the workbench.

What are you going to carve for a design? That's up to you. Usually, a

47 • **Stylized vine design.**

48 • **A more involved vine.**

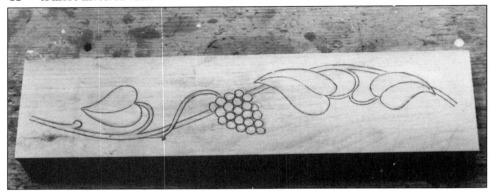

major stem or branch runs the length of the board, with some type of floral scroll branching from it: lilac leaves for the Friendship; oak leaves and acorns, signifying strength; or just an attractive convoluted pattern.

Vine (Incised)

For want of a better word, let's call the type of leaf scroll (and similar designs) used on most trailboards, a vine. Figure 47 shows the type of leaf forms used on a Friendship, and one assumes that the carver who originated this design started with a lilac leaf. You can carve it all with one U-gouge or veiner, or leave off the berries and do it all with a V-gouge or a knife. Traditionally, the carved-in lines were painted dark green on a white background. No one says that you have to stop there; you can add to the design as in Figures 48 and 51, or however you like.

If you want to design your own carving but don't know how to start, follow a procedure such as this: Lay out an undulate line on your trailboard pattern,

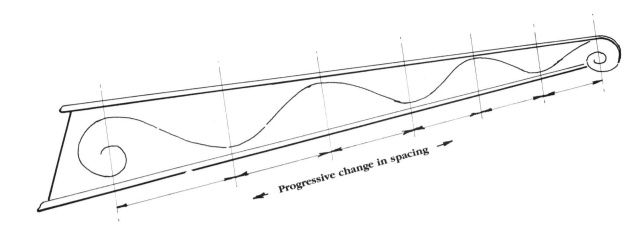

49 • Basic undulate line.

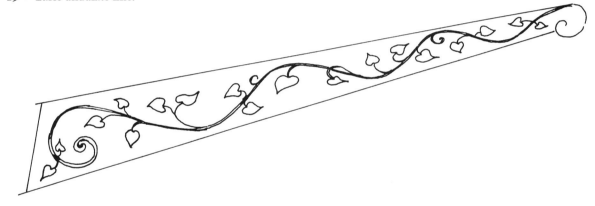

50 • Design elements added.

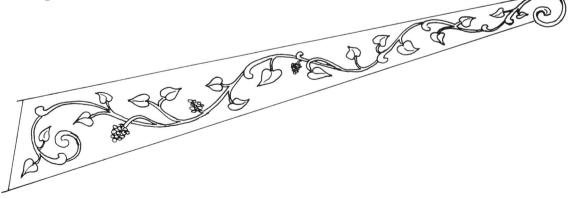

51 • Further additions.

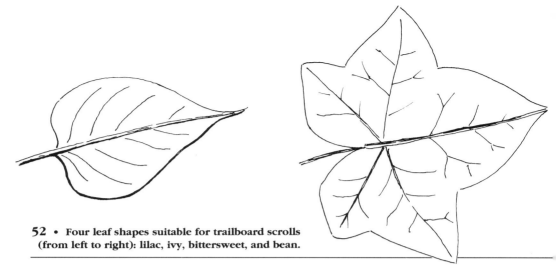

52 • **Four leaf shapes suitable for trailboard scrolls (from left to right): lilac, ivy, bittersweet, and bean.**

following the central idea of Figure 49. Some people find it easiest to do this at full size; others do a scale drawing and then enlarge it. The important thing is to make the curves free-flowing and graceful. This line will be the main stem of your design, be it ivy, a grapevine, oak leaves, or whatever.

Using an actual plant leaf or one of the illustrations here (see Figure 52), simplify the leaf's shape to a modified heart, as shown, or draw a more factual or interesting shape. Lilacs certainly don't have berries, so perhaps you'd rather use a bittersweet leaf, which does, or a grape leaf (Figure 53), so you can have a whole cluster of grapes. Or, stop with just the stem and leaves (see Figure 50)—a very simple vine, but there will be plenty of Friendship sloops to keep you company.

53 • **Basic elements of a grape design.**

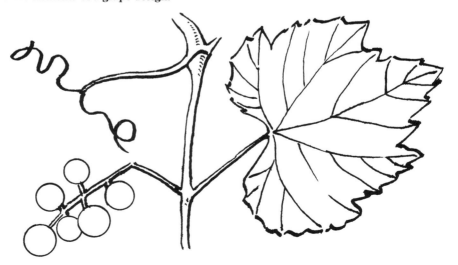

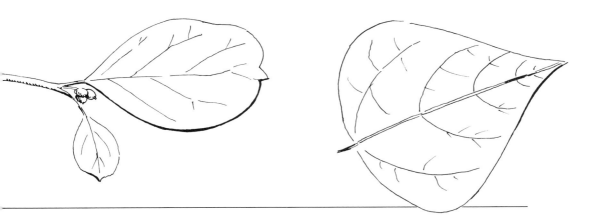

If that's too simple, add some more elements, as shown in Figure 51. First, break up the vine with some stylized buds; then add some berries. If you still aren't content, draw the leaves in a more factual manner, and use the tendrils to wind around and fill in the blank spaces. Make a real vine out of it, but stay with your original line.

Figure 54 shows the factual elements of an oak design. Use the same type of basic line to start with—even though we both know that acorns don't grow on a vine. Simplify, stylize, distort, bend the leaves over and under—do what you wish to make the design graceful and interesting. Use someone else's design as a basis for ideas if you must, but don't copy it slavishly; create your own.

54 • **Basic elements of a white oak leaf design.**

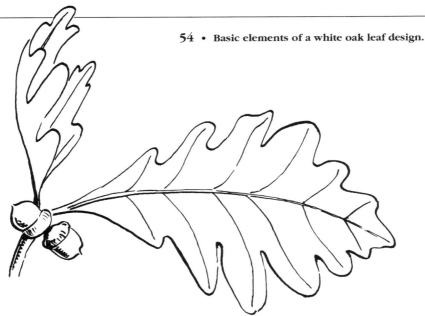

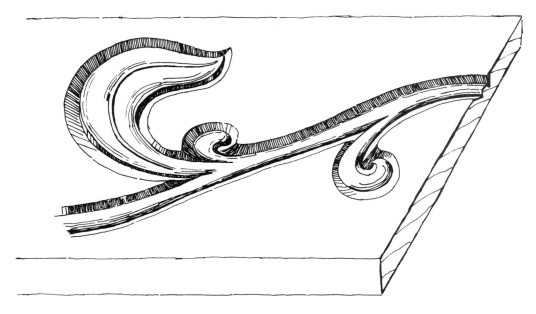

55 • **The simple way to carve a bas-relief.**

An Oak Leaf Design (Bas-Relief)

Incised carving is easier to do than relief carving, but not as rich-looking, so if you want your trailboard carving in relief, the easiest way is to outline the design with V-cuts and round the internal parts (Figure 55). For true bas-relief on a small board, you must recess all of the background. This, of course,

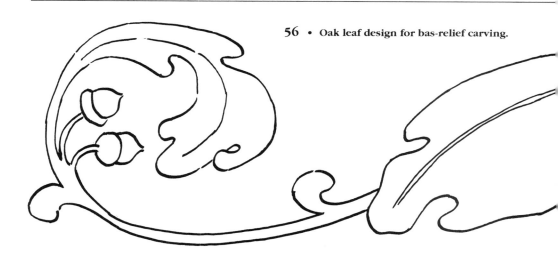

56 • **Oak leaf design for bas-relief carving.**

means that you must start with adequate thickness so that the final piece will not be too thin. The total height of the carving should not project beyond the rails, or there will be no way to protect pieces from being knocked off by lines, boathooks, and so forth.

Figure 56 shows a simple oak leaf design to be done in relief with some of the steps shown here. First, transfer the design to a board 3/4 inch thick (Figure 57). Next, draw a line around the edge of the board, not quite halfway down, to define the background level (Figure 58). Roughly outline the design—about 1/16 inch away from the lines, and using a U-gouge—to make a stop-cut. Next, starting from the outer edges and cutting across the grain, rough away the background (this is called "grounding"). The next step is to go around again with a number 3 or other reasonably flat gouge to smooth up the ground; at the same time, you can set in the design outline with chisels and gouges. Once you have roughed away the ground, the chisel can cut straight down instead of being forced back, because of its bevel, into the design. (See Figure 60a.)

If there are thin stems, such as at the acorns in this design, don't worry about getting all the way down to the background between them, and don't pry out chips; it's too easy to break the thin sections this way. You can work the background down as you go along—just be sure to keep the design defined.

Once you have smoothed the ground, begin molding the shapes, not finishing any one unit but determining what is going to go under or over, what grows out of where, what is high and what low (Figure 59). Define the roundness of the shapes.

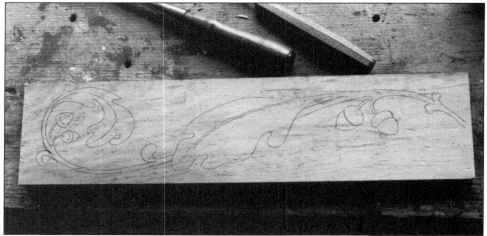

57 • **Design on the board.**

58 • **Outline stop-cut made and rough grounding started.**

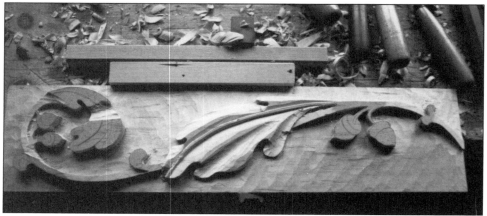

59 • **Starting to mold shapes.**

Now for the enjoyment. Begin finish-molding the shapes, rounding the stems and making the buds grow (Figure 61). Use all of your gouges, flat and skew chisels, whatever tool fits the need. Always keep the grain in mind; it's easy to get so interested in folding part of a leaf over a stem that you forget the way the grain is running and split off a piece. Don't despair if it happens; you can redesign the leaf to fit the wood that's left (leaves grow in all sizes!).

If the work begins to look too hard to do—or, for that matter, too easy—I heartily recommend that you find and study a photo of Grinling Gibbons's panels (a book about Gibbons and other traditional English shipcarvers is listed under "What to Look For, and Where," at the back of this book). I'll swear that you can pick his

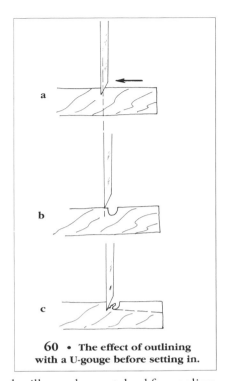

60 • **The effect of outlining with a U-gouge before setting in.**

flowers, and I don't believe his Cosima panel will ever be matched for realism and undercutting. Of course, his kind of carving would never do on a boat. The rule here is not to make things too fragile or too undercut.

You don't necessarily have to make the background perfectly flat. Leave the tool marks in if you wish. If this treatment of showing tool marks doesn't please you for the leaves, stems, etc., go ahead and smooth them up with sandpaper.

61 • **Carving almost done.**

62 • Carving a trailboard design in relief. The design has been cut
out of separate pieces and glued and nailed to the background.

63 • The bow of the schooner *Bill of Rights.*
This is the trailboard being worked on in Figure 62.

On large boards, to avoid cutting away a great amount of background, you can roughly saw the design out of another board, using a bandsaw. When I've done this, I've broken up the design into segments, for two reasons: One, you can get the grain to run more consistently with the design; two, it takes far less wood. Then trace the design onto the background, and glue and nail the pieces to it. Use waterproof glue and finish nails. Don't sink the nails, as you'll want to pull them out for the carving operation. After carving, they can be replaced and sunk for added strength. This is the process that was followed for the schooner *Bill of Rights*. Figure 62 shows one of her trailboards being carved; Figure 63 shows the finished bow. The shield was the trademark for the vessel, and at the owner's request one was carved to fold around the stemhead.

On large work you can carve the face of the rails with a channel, cove, or beading, if you wish.

When the trailboards are complete and fastened to the hull, fit the billethead decoration. Again, I would emphasize that lines from the trailboard flow into and terminate at the billethead. Avoid any appearance of a "stuck-on" billethead.

Head carvings are a major item of a vessel's appearance, so spend time on the design. The final results are too important to permit skimpy initial considerations.

10 • Stern Eagles and Other Birds

From the very early days of this country, the American eagle in realistic or stylized form has probably graced more transoms than any other ornament. If you want tradition, the eagle is it. You can arch a name-board over him, with a port-of-call board below, or the eagle can carry a lettered banner in his beak or claws. Design your own eagle or find a design in an old book (see "What to Look For, and Where"), on a government seal, or in an advertisement. Whatever you do, you should carve all of his lines strongly.

If you don't care to make this positive a statement (I heard that phrase on a news broadcast), carve a seagull, a duck (Figure 64), or even a dove. After all, the latter is what Noah sent out from the Ark to see if there was a landfall to be

64 • A duck used as a transom ornament.

65 • **Stylized eagle carved by John Haley Bellamy.**

made anywhere. Almost any of the seabirds will make a good motif.

Whatever bird you decide to carve, avoid making thin, cross-grained parts. Tuck a thin beak over some other part of the bird; use undercutting to make something appear thin; or, if your design doesn't permit this, carve the whole thing in relief on an oval board, using the board background as a support. Study the design well before starting, and work out the carving in your mind.

Ideally, your design should be a recognizable motif or unit, even from a distance. You don't want someone banging into your boat because he was trying to figure out what's on your transom instead of looking where he was going.

Because the carving is on a transom, which is usually curved, the same mounting problems occur that we spoke about in Chapter 4, "Sternboards," in the section on "Fitting the Board to the Transom." No steam bending will solve the problem here, but it is possible that a mild hollowing of the board back will produce a good fit. If the transom has an excessive curve, you will either have to add wood at the ends or resort to a thicker piece.

I once had to carve a 6-foot eagle for a 65-foot yacht with a canoe stern. This was done by making a template of the bulwark area to be occupied by the bird. Light pine boards were scribed to fit the top and bottom lines of the bulwarks; these were then connected by verticals that were cut to fit the slight up-and-down curvature. The whole contraption was then removed from the boat and taken to the shop. There I built a rugged framework that fit the pattern (Figure 66), so in effect I had a section of bulwark to fit the bird to, and at the same time I had a jig for holding it while carving. This same procedure can be followed no matter what size your carving will be. It ensures a good match to the hull. Do the shaping of the back first; don't carve a bird or

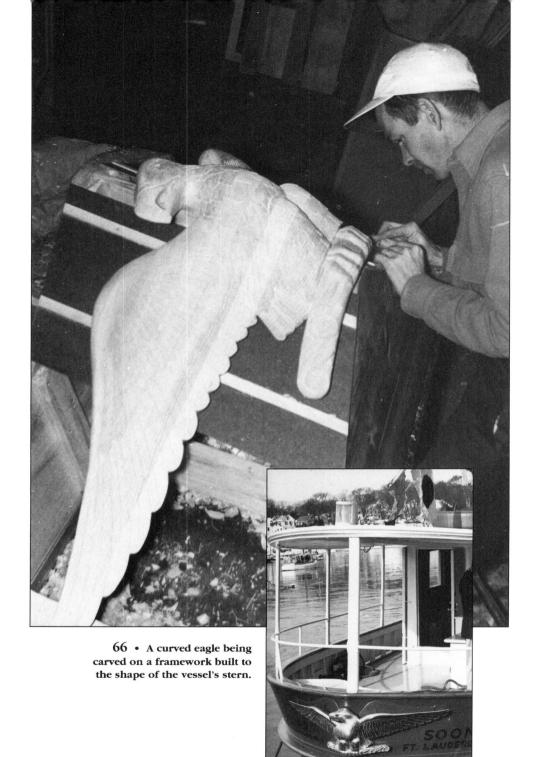

66 • A curved eagle being
carved on a framework built to
the shape of the vessel's stern.

something and then try to shape the back—it's too difficult.

Making the block for a large carving like this can sometimes tax your ingenuity. This one was done with layered 2-by-6's, alternately crossed and lapped over in the middle for strength. The pieces were held together with Weldwood glue and dowels. The plank positions were laid out on the eagle drawing so that the pieces could be roughed out on the bandsaw. Starting with the four largest pieces, they were drilled for dowels and glued and clamped together. When this assembly was dry, more pieces were added to the top and bottom in the same way. Care was taken in locating the dowels so that they would all be under the surface of the finished carving. This method of forming the block gave me a lot of crossing end grain in the middle, but it was rugged and used the minimum of wood.

Any large carving—bow or stern, bird, animal or human—will have to be built up. Use your head in constructing the block. Don't fasten pieces together with screws unless you are sure that you won't hit them in the process of carving. Don't have joints in a position where they will hold water. Try to keep the design from having protruding fragile parts. If you must have, say, an extended arm on a figure or an olive branch in a bird's beak, it is well if the construction is designed so that these pieces can be added on and even removed, if necessary. In case of breakage, it's an easier matter to replace them.

If the back of the bird is to be flat, there's no problem. Hold the work on the bench with a carver's screw or padded clamps. If you haven't acquired a bench screw, read in Chapter 13, "Tools and Sharpening," about making one. I use clamps to hold the work during all of the heavy roughing out, and I then use one bench screw in the center of the bird. This permits me to rotate the work, making carving easier, and to vary the angle of the lighting.

The Eagle

For this next project, an eagle for the stern—or a wall, if you wish—we'll use photos and sketches of an eagle carved from the design in Figure 67. The original of this was about 28 inches long and carved from a pine plank 1-1/2 inches by 9-1/2 inches. If your wood is 1-3/4 inches thick, all the better; there is nothing hard and fast about the thickness requirement—or any of the dimensions, for that matter.

If you have completed the previous, simpler carvings in this book, there is no need to repeat an explanation of the handling of tools. You will, of course, block out the carving to rough shape, establishing the levels—that is, the thickness at different places on the bird—that you want (see Figure 68). After that, you can carve as simply or in as much detail as you wish.

I like to finish the eye first because its appearance is critical and because it

67 • **A design for an eagle.**

puts life in the bird. If you spoil it or don't like its looks, the eye can be re-carved without doing over the whole head. You can see from Figures 74 and 76 that this is a very simple eye; the pupil is nothing but a dome-shaped circle with a center concave recess. The famous marine carver John Haley Bellamy (1836–1914), who did so much to stylize the carving of eagles, used what some people call a "tube" eyeball (see Figures 65 and 69). It's very dramatic. Whatever style you use, with the completed eye to keep watch on what you're doing, it's easier to keep the rest of your carving alive. And, of course, it's someone to talk to as you carve: a benevolent eye approving your praise when the chips peel off as they should, and a glittering, fierce one to receive your muttered curses when a feather splits. Forgive the old carver his strange ways, but things like this do happen when you work alone.

As feathers make up most of the surface, you should consider how you want to show them. They overlap much as fish scales do, from top to bottom;

so after roughing the levels, you should cut in the various rows of feathers—
working from the top down—so as to produce an effect of curving clapboards
(see Figure 70). When you have done this, redraw the individual feathers and
shape them with their overlaps or steps. Actually, not even this need be done;
you can just carve the sweeping, hollowed curve of the wing surface and
outline a feather pattern with a veiner. A stylized eagle is treated in this way.
John Bellamy made some stylized eagle plaques that are models of simplicity.
Only a few oversized feathers are outlined on the wings. All of the grace and
beauty of the bird is expressed by the overall form, not by details.

Unless the complete design is simplified, I would carve the rows of feathers
as I described in the paragraph above. But again, there is a choice. A simple
and very effective treatment is shown in Figure 71. The center spine of each
feather is simply a narrow V- or U-groove, and random notches are cut into
the feather edges to indicate breaks in the barbs.

68 • **An eagle roughed out to establish the levels.**

However, I have also seen examples of eagle carvings in which each feather was elaborately detailed. The surfaces were waved at the edges and looked soft. Even if you don't wish to go this far, you can carve the spine to appear raised (which it really is) and put in some fine V-cuts to show the pattern of the barbs (Figure 72). Perhaps the best way is to try various methods on a piece of scrap, and then decide which one you want to use. Don't count the feathers, though, or you'll decide to leave them all blank! And don't go to the extreme of burning in all the barb lines, as is done with the decoy bird carvings that you see in exhibits. Your bird won't be viewed from close enough to have this treatment appreciated, and it's too fragile a surface for marine use.

The beak and lower jaw are, of course, smooth and are carved oversize, with the backs of these parts distorted in depth to give them the necessary strength (see Figure 74). The eagle's head and throat look well if treated as hair, with closely spaced grooves made with a veiner. The thighs may be done the same way or covered with small feathers. In our example, the leading-edge wing feathers were treated as the head was, using a veiner to give more of a downy look (Figure 73). They could instead be small feathers carved in the same style as the rest of the wing, or they could even be left

78

smooth. The feet and legs are rather knobby, with rings running around them. The claws or "toenails" are like the beak—very smooth.

In our example, I separated the ribbon into front and back sections where it went through the beak, but for use on a boat it would be stronger, if not as nice-looking, if it were left solid. If the folds in the ribbon bother you, take a piece of cloth and pinch it as it would be if held in the beak, and see how it looks. The way the ribbon folds at the ends shouldn't cause you trouble if you've carved nameboards as described earlier. Look at the photos (Figure 68 shows it best), and notice the way the ribbon slopes on the face of the carving—don't keep the ribbon parallel to the back of the board, but vary the surface.

You'll have to turn the bird over once in a while to make the sloping-edge relief cuts. For this reason, I left the four highest points (the wing "elbows" and the highest parts of the ribbons) at block thickness until almost the end, and used them as clamping points. Put an old piece of padded material, such as quilting, between the bench and the carving face to fully protect the face when working on the back.

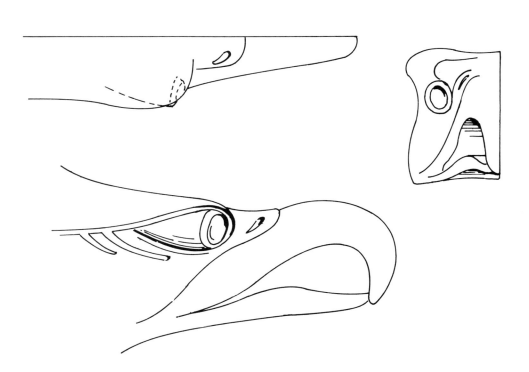

69 • **Eagle head with "tube" eyeball.**

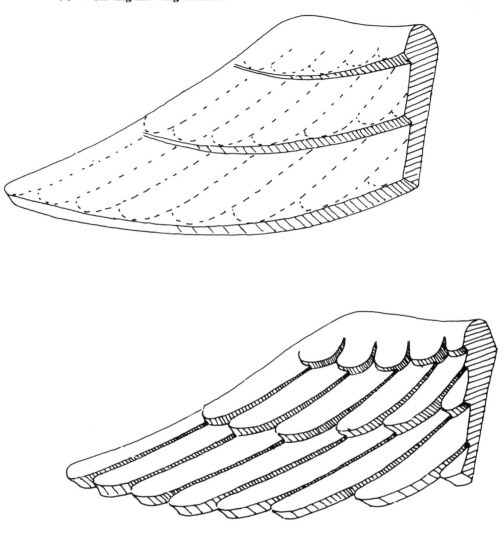

The ribbon offers quite a bit of room for whatever lettering you wish. If the eagle is going on a transom, you may want to carve in the boat's name and port of call, or perhaps thirteen stars. For a pure decoration you could use Commander Lawrence's famous "Don't give up the ship" or the 1812 slogan "Free trade and sailors' rights." These belligerent sayings go well with this eagle, as he is carrying only the arrows and not the olive branch.

71 • A simple treatment of feathers.

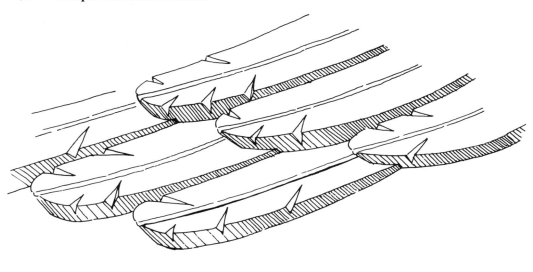

72 • A more elaborate treatment of feathers.

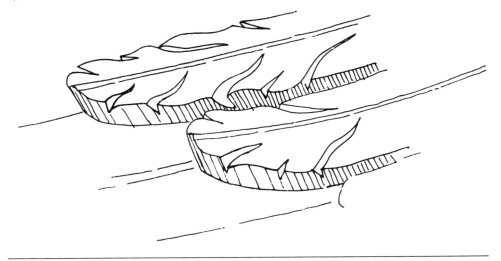

Wood Defects, and What to Do About Them

Figures 74 and 75 illustrate some repairs that were made in the wood. For this eagle I deliberately used an old piece of pine with a knot and some worm holes, so that I could describe repairs. Two of the worm holes appeared on the ribbon face, but I ignored them until the roughing-out was done. At this point two rough plugs were jammed into the holes for centers and then

73 • A veiner can give the leading edges of the wings a downy look.

74 • Two worm holes that require repairs on the ribbon face.

75 • Plugs glued in the drilled-out worm holes. These plugs will be pared down flush.

76 • The finished carving, ready for banner decorations and painting.

77 • **The painted eagle—the way I chose to finish it.**

drilled out with a 1/2-inch drill. Two round plugs were then made from some of the scrap sawn off during the initial shaping of the bird, with the grain running across the plug face. With the plugs and holes well coated with glue, the plugs were tapped into place, with the grain running in the same direction as the surrounding wood. The next day the plugs were cut off flush, and, when the final shaping of the ribbon was completed, they were hardly noticeable. In another area, where a worm had made a U-shaped gouge in the surface, I used a plastic wood filler, making sure beforehand that I had removed all loose dust from the worm's boring.

The knot disappeared in the carving process, leaving only some wild grain that called for careful carving in that area. So don't despair if you find poor areas in your carving block. Work around them if you can; if you can't, cut them out and replace the wood.

Once again, I'd like to comment on how you do these carvings. They should be expressions of yourself, so anything said in these pages is suggestion only. Follow the drawing in Figure 67 if you wish, but if you argue with the way I do something, fine—do it your way. Design your own bird, think up a new way to do the feathers, and if you carve more than one eagle, make them different. If you like realism, visit the nearest museum that has mounted specimens, and study them. If this doesn't appeal to you, go the other way— simplify to the point where the bird's character is demonstrated by planes and outline. However you do it, carving is more than just a manual skill.

You can take other bird designs from illustrations in bird books and apply much the same carving techniques as described here. A swimming duck or similar design need not have individual feathers portrayed; a better plan is to carve according to prominent color separations or whatever makes the bird look distinctive. Look through books on carving duck decoys for tips, but do not go into the detail that the master decoy carvers of today use. For marine work, things should be rugged and simple.

78 • The bronze figurehead for the Pemaquid-type Friendship sloop *Old Baldy* (above) was cast from a wood carving. A duplicate casting (below) has been mounted as a bookend.

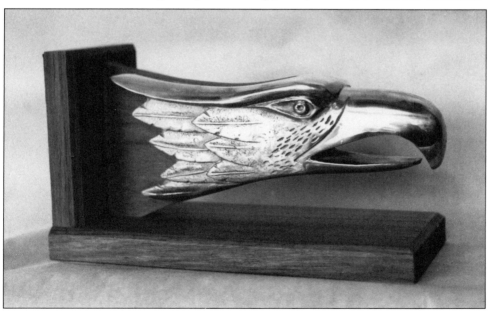

11 · Other Uses of Decorative Carving

Where else can you use carvings? Almost anywhere your heart desires. Some Dutch yachts have carvings everywhere, from the stem to the top of the rudderhead. During World War II, Nazi Air Marshal Hermann Goering ordered a yacht built in a Dutch yard, but he never received delivery because she was never quite finished. Part of the clever Dutch delaying tactics must have been the amount of carving aboard, which is almost like 17th-century carving in its profusion, making the cabin of *Groote Beer* (Figure 79) elegant and decorative beyond belief.

Tillers have long been favorite objects for carving. The inboard end of the tiller—where your hand rests—and the knob at the very end are frequently served, or wound with line in some manner, so as to form an antislip device and decoration. These effects can be made permanent by carving the tiller as though it were served. I once saw a French cutter with a tiller so carved, and the result was a real conversation piece, as well as being useful. The grip was carved as coxcombing and was finished off at the ends with carved Turk's Head knots. The knob carving simulated a Monkey's Fist knot, which is the knot used on a heaving line. A lot of careful work was required to make this tiller, but it was something I'd like to have on our boat. Maybe someday when there's time.... If this interests you, obtain a copy of one of Hervey Garrett Smith's books, such as *The Arts of the Sailor* or *The Marlinspike Sailor*. Smith's drawings of decorative rope coverings look real, and they are a good

79 • Fanciful friezes of squid and other sea creatures (top and above right) decorate the companionway of *Groote Beer* ("Great Bear"), a Dutch botter-jacht built in the 1940s. A "fish" handrail (above left) and a gearbox (right) are two more examples of Anton Fortuin's extensive carvings.

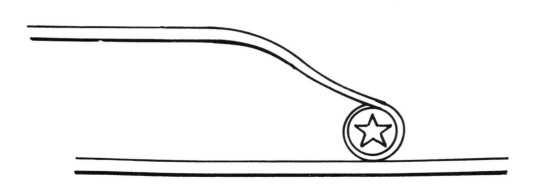

80 • Simple rail endings.

guide for this type of carving. If you have the time, six-stranded coach whip-ping is ideal. The knob could be carved as a dolphin's head, a human head, or any other round object that appeals to you.

In the days when sailing vessels had several levels of decks, the rails ended gracefully in scrolls, ogees, or other carvings. If your boat has rail endings, this is another area where you can show your skills. Some suggestions are

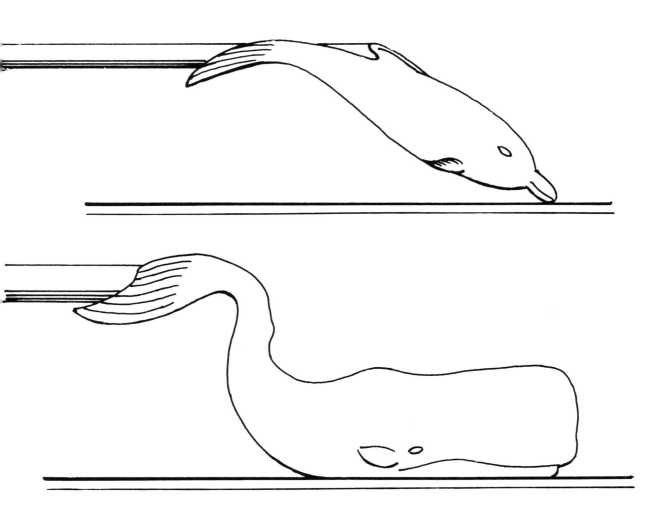

81 • More elaborate rail endings.

shown in Figures 80 and 81. The same type of carving can be done on the after ends of the cockpit coaming.

Some yachts today still carry catheads for anchors, and these can be finished on the end with a cat's head, as were catheads on the 19th-century yachts. "Cat" in this case usually means a lion. The ever-popular star is also a traditional ending.

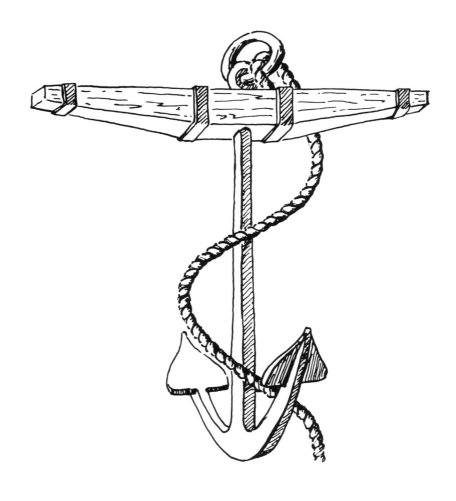

82 • An anchor motif.

Afloat or ashore, sea chests are attractive items of furniture, and bas-relief carvings of a nautical theme on their tops add a great deal to their appeal. You can use the plan in Figure 85 to build a sea chest, carving decorations on the pieces before assembly. The cupboard door panels in either the galley or the kitchen are other places for marine carving. An anchor (Figure 82), a house flag, or other simple design sketched with a veiner will do. I can just see the enthusiast standing in the middle of his kitchen, gouge in hand, a wild look in his eye, thinking, "What can I do next?" Enjoy yourself, but have a little restraint.

83 • Imaginative carvings can really brighten up a boat. *Ouderhoek*, a traditional Dutch sailing vessel, has an alligator on the rudderhead (left) and fish on the ends of the bulwarks (below).

84 • One of a pair of whimsical oarlock pads carved by Dave LeFebvre of Seattle, Washington, for a rowboat.

TOP OF COVER TO BE DECORATED
WITH COLONIAL EAGLE - APPROX. 18" WINGSPREAD

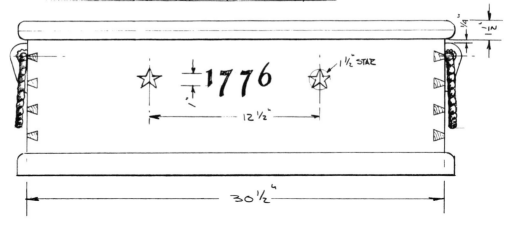

☆ 1776 ☆ 1½" STAR

12½"

30½"

¼"

1"

THESE 3 VIEWS - 3" = 1' SCALE
ALL MATERIAL ¾" PINE EXCEPT AS NOTED

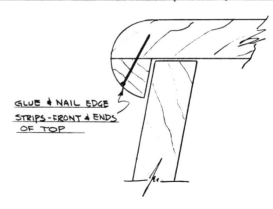

GLUE & NAIL EDGE
STRIPS - FRONT & ENDS
OF TOP

SCREWED & PLUGGED

ALTERNATE CORNER
CONSTRUCTION

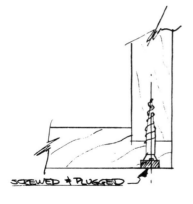

⅝ DIA.
1" DIA.
30°

LEATHER WASHER   4 REQ.

ALTERNATE HANDLES
DECORATIVE ROPE WORK
NOT TO SCALE

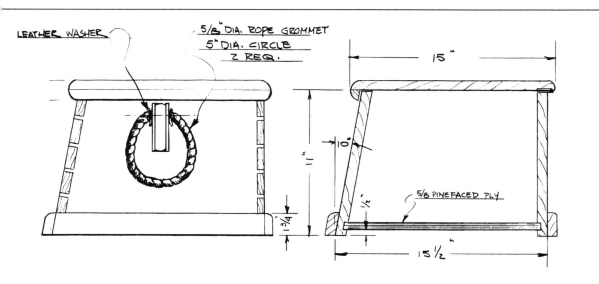

LEATHER WASHER

5/8" DIA. ROPE GROMMET
5" DIA. CIRCLE
2 REQ.

15"

10°

5/8 PINEFACED PLY

1/2"

1 3/4

11"

15 1/2"

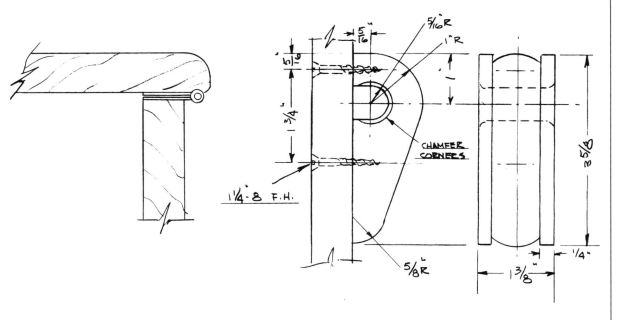

5/16"R

1"R

5/16"

5/16"

1 3/4"

CHAMFER
CORNERS

1 1/4 - 8 F.H.

5/8"R

3 5/8

1/4"

1 3/8"

GROMMET CLEAT - 2 REQ.

FINISH - EITHER NATURAL
OLD WOOD STAIN OR ANTIQUED
GREEN PAINT

85 • **A sea chest as a basis for carving.**

12 · Finishes

I have mentioned finishes previously, but a little elaboration on the subject might help. We already know that light and shadow emphasize the efforts that you put into a carving. Suppose that you had a house nameboard on which the letters had not come out quite as smoothly as you wanted. The board will be read quite close up—it's not meant to stop traffic—so contrast between letters and board is not of prime importance. Staining the board a medium brown and painting the letters buff or a dark tone will minimize the unevenness of carving. The flatter the paint, the more the carved surface will flatten. A semi-gloss paint will allow a few highlights, and a gloss paint even more, so you can subdue to any degree the apparent surface roughness. Working the other way, the lighter the color and the higher the gloss finish, the more every carved surface and line will show its shape. The ultimate in richness is gold leaf.

Quarter boards and such look well when finished bright with several thin coats of varnish sanded between coats. Take care to brush out any varnish puddles in the letters, and in sanding be careful not to round the sharp top edges of the letters. After the varnish is dry and hard (wait at least twenty-four hours after applying the last coat), paint the letters, again watching for puddles.

If your boat sports no brightwork whatever, your feeling being that it is too gaudy, substitute paint for the varnish. A black board with yellow carving looks good as long as you subdue the yellow a bit, toward a buff color. Yellow is, of course, the poor man's gold and has been used extensively over the years.

The carvings on your transom or on your billethead and trailboards can be emphasized with some color if you wish, but don't overdo it. Any national motifs such as shields, flags, and stars can use red, white, and blue, of course. Old-time figureheads were frequently painted in colors, so the tradition is established, but please remember that they were a small ornament on a very large hull. Catch the observer's eye, but don't blind it.

Gold Leaf

Gold leafing may be a time-consuming process, but once you've rowed out to your boat in the morning and seen the water-reflected light rippling across the carving, all the effort will be worth it. Gold leaf is pure gold beaten out so thinly that pieces of it will float in the air. Don't use "gold" paint or powders: They are not true gold, and they turn brown after short exposure to weather. Leaf comes in little books and can be purchased as "loose" or "patent." Loose is exactly that—a sheet of gold between pages and free to be picked out. Patent gold for "gilding in the wind" is slightly adhered to a backing sheet and is much easier for the beginner to handle and use. If you are working outside, it's a must. Visit your local paint or art store or a sign painter to purchase gold leaf. You may want to check first about the cost. Be warned that gold leaf is real gold, and its price goes up rapidly when the gold market rises.

A good, smooth surface is needed for gold leafing, and this is best provided by a marine enamel. The enamel can be almost any color, but yellow is preferred. Gold size, a slow-drying, varnish-type finish, is then brushed on smoothly and evenly. You can tell when the size has dried to the right tack by testing it with a knuckle. If it sticks to your knuckle, it's not dry enough; you should feel a slight pull and hear a light tick as you pull your knuckle away. Pick up a sheet of patent gold by the backing paper and lay it face down on the size. Rub the back of the paper evenly so that the gold adheres to the size when you lift off the backing. Continue this method, overlapping the sheets slightly. Any missed spots can be covered the same way. The next day, when the size is hard, burnish the surface (rub it gently) with absorbent cotton to polish and remove any excess gold. Do not varnish or otherwise try to finish over the gold, as this will kill its brilliance. Gold will outlast the rest of the finish, but be sure to seal and paint or varnish the back of the board as well as the front, so that no moisture can get in.

Applying loose-leaf gold requires skill but is the fastest method for covering large areas. Loose-leaf gold can only be used indoors in still air. Preparation for gilding is the same as above, except that the handling of the gold sheet is different. The gilder uses a "tip," a soft brush the width of the gold sheet. The tip is gently brushed over the gilder's hair to mildly charge it with static electricity, and is then touched to one edge of the gold sheet. The gold can then be lifted and floated over to the work. Place the sheets so that they overlap slightly. Don't allow the tip to touch the size or become sticky in any way, or the gold won't let go. If you've been using fish oil to hold your hair in place, maybe you'd better stand under the shower before trying this method.

Gold leaf is also available in rolls of different widths for striping. This might be the most economical way for the beginner to gild letters.

You can now buy fake gold leaf made of plastic. The temptation to use it is strong because the price is so much more affordable than that of real gold. I would not recommend it for marine use because the one example I've seen lost its lustre and turned a rather unpleasant color before one sailing season was over. It could be my lack of skill with a different medium, but I also found it much more difficult to lay down an even covering with it.

13 · Tools and Sharpening

If you have progressed to carving eagles and other reasonably large and complicated subjects and have found it interesting, then you will also have developed the wish to acquire more tools. At this stage of the game, the long list of available tools will not scare you away from the whole idea of carving, because your experience will guide you in determining what you need.

There are really only four types of carving tools—flat, U-shaped, V-shaped, or square-sided U—but by grinding or shaping them differently, the manufacturers come up with eight tools (Figure 86). There are five variants of these that make carving easier (Figure 87). Each of these variants comes in about a dozen sizes—that is, if you can find a place that sells them all.

The gouges also come in varying degrees of curvature, or sweeps, from almost flat up to half-round; and you can purchase V-gouges with cutting edges that form various included angles. The various shapes are made to simplify problems that arise in carving. An obvious example is the bottom of a recessed area: You can carve it smoothly with a bent gouge, whereas a straight gouge would only dig into the wood. And, of course, a short bent gouge will get into an even smaller place. Short bent gouges require a different hand motion than you have been using with straight gouges, and you probably will find them more difficult to use for this reason. Instead of trying to push with the right hand, use the left for the forward motion and do some of the steering with the right. It's difficult to describe, but knowing that the hands have to reverse their roles somewhat will start you on the right course.

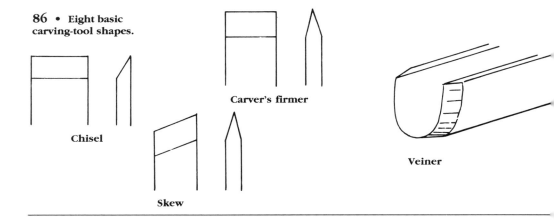

86 • Eight basic carving-tool shapes.

Carver's firmer

Chisel

Veiner

Skew

Go slowly at first—don't try to remove too much wood at a time—and you will teach yourself how to do it.

Back-bent gouges are used for undercutting rounds (like grapes) and are not often needed.

Short bent skews (left and right) are a great help in grounding, for reaching into acutely angled corners.

Fishtails are designed with a narrow shank to give them more clearance for cutting in confined areas. For some unknown reason, I find them a great pleasure to use, and sometimes it seems easier to get good results with them than with an ordinary straight gouge.

A good tool catalog such as Garrett Wade Company's or Wood Carver's Supply, Inc.'s (see "What to Look For, and Where") illustrates nicely the various shapes and sweeps of the many tools available.

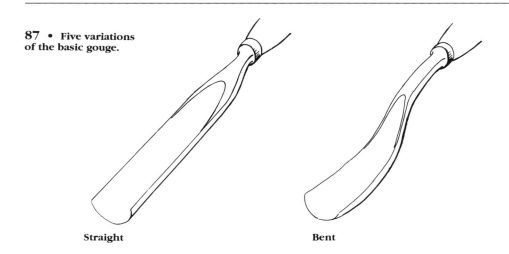

87 • Five variations of the basic gouge.

Straight

Bent

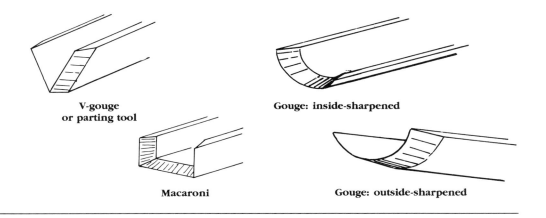

**V-gouge
or parting tool**

Gouge: inside-sharpened

Macaroni

Gouge: outside-sharpened

Most of us who enjoy working with our hands like tools, myself included. Even if I seldom use some of them, they are there to do a particular job when needed, and I delight in the way that a certain tool does that job. Besides, good tools have a functional beauty. Now, if someone were to present me with a complete set of all shapes and sizes of carving tools, I'd feel as if I had the riches of the world; I'd make fancy drawers in a chest to keep them in. I also know from past experience that some of them would never be used. The truth is, you develop a liking for and a skill with certain tools, and you find ways to use them in preference to others. This is due partly to the feel of the handle and partly to the temper of the tool. All carving tools seem to vary in their ability to hold an edge. I have some gouges that stay sharp no matter how many knots I cut through, and others that in spite of retempering just can't cut with the smoothness I like.

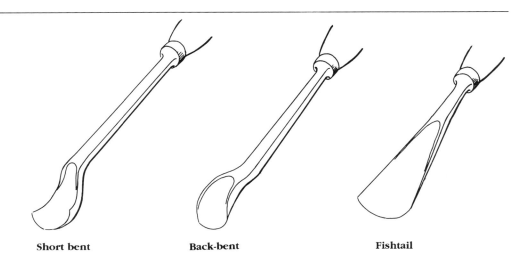

Short bent

Back-bent

Fishtail

You'll need various gouge sizes, but to buy them all would be foolish. You'd spend so much time picking up one and putting it down to pick up another that nothing would get done. It's quicker to take a second cut with the one in your hand.

So you're serious about carving and want a good, all-around collection to work with? My choice would resemble the following:

Chisels and firmers—5mm, 12mm, 25mm

Skew firmers—5mm, 16mm

Skew short bent chisels—5mm, 12mm (one right-handed and one left-handed of each size)

Gouges (straight)—5mm, 10mm, 25mm (one inside-sharpened and one outside-sharpened of each size—about a number 9 sweep, a little less than half round)

Gouges (fishtail)—8mm, 14mm (number 5)

Gouges (veiner)—1mm, 5mm (number 11)

Gouges (V-parting)—3mm, 10mm (number 12)

As you get used to these tools, you'll find that certain ones work well for you, and so you'll wish to acquire more sizes of that type.

Sometimes, unexpected tools work best. The daughter of a long-deceased boatbuilder was cleaning out his shop and sold me a 2-inch slick and a 2-1/2-inch shallow gouge. A slick is a chisel blade of quite some size with a turned-up handle socket; this means that the bottom or flat of the blade can stay flat on a surface with the handle up out of the way. A slick should be fitted with a long handle, but mine had just a stump left. I was carving a great many half-models for builders at the time, and these two tools became my favorites. They had enough size and weight for excellent control, and they would take such a fine edge without breaking that I could use them as planes. It was a pleasure to see the paper-thin chips one could take off, using these tools.

So, acquire your tools where you can. They certainly don't need to be a matched set. Once you have them, don't throw them in a drawer to rattle together. As you've found out by this time, the best steel is no good if it's dull, and having loose tools bumping into one another is a quick way to dull and nick them. Some carvers keep their tools in a cloth case for protection, but I prefer shallow drawers with wooden holders or partitions to keep them separate.

Along with the carving tools, you may want to acquire some of the helpful aids, one of which is the mallet (see Figure 88). This style of mallet is preferred over the kind that looks like a hammer, because it always hits the tool handle in the same way. If a flat-faced mallet were used and the face were not exactly square to the tool handle, it would knock the tool sideways. Try it;

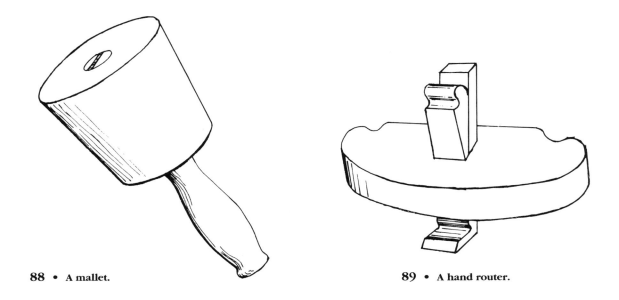

88 • **A mallet.**

89 • **A hand router.**

you'll see. You can buy beautiful lignum-vitae mallets, or, if you have a lathe, you can make your own. Mine came from a small maple log (out of the fire-wood stack) and a piece of locust that had been used as a handle for some tool a long time ago. You'll want enough weight in the mallet so that you don't have to pound with it.

If you will be carving bas-relief panels that have large, recessed flat areas, a hand router (Figure 89) can be a benefit. Again, one of these may be purchased or made.

90 • **A flat "cramp."**

91 • **A carver's screw.**

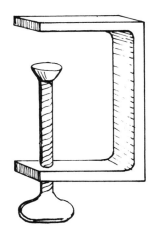

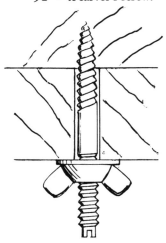

For holding work to the bench, you can use ordinary screen turn-buttons, bench holdfasts, C-clamps, or, better yet, what the English call "flat cramps," which don't stick up and get in your way (Figure 90). Large work (such as an eagle) can best be held by carvers' screws through the bench top (Figure 91). These can also be purchased or made. Mine are 1/4-inch-diameter lag screws, long enough to go through a loose hole in the bench top and penetrate the work about 3/4 inch, with another 3/4 inch or so extending below the underside of the bench. Cut the head off the lag, and thread the shank for a 1/4-inch wing nut. The end of the shank should have a screwdriver slot hack-sawn in it. If this is beyond your tool capabilities, go to your local hardware shop and look for the screw bolts used to fasten down toilet seats. With a wing nut, they might be long enough to do the job.

When doing the fox head for the schooner *John F. Leavitt*, I had great difficulty in holding the piece after the shape was roughed out. It was of large size, and design requirements made it a rather round shape. A couple of bags made from light canvas and sewn shut after being partially filled with sand solved the problem (see Figure 92). With them placed on the bench, the carving could be settled down onto them and clamped in place.

Years ago, my grandfather had a summer cottage in Maine. One fall, he failed to get a bill from the caretaker for the year's maintenance work. He wrote the old gentleman to inquire what he owed. (They were both State-of-

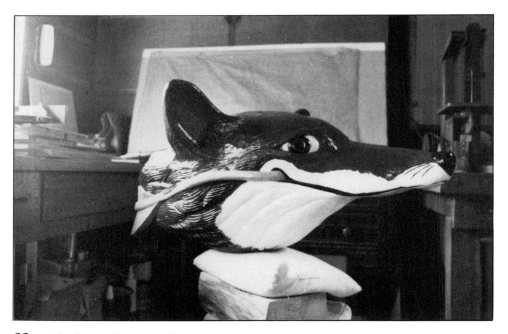

92 • **The fox resting on sandbags.**

Mainers and therefore very honest in their dealings with each other.) The answer came back, "I have lost the stick I stir my desk up with, can't find an account." This is all right for a desk—it's certainly the way mine looks—but please, keep your edged tools separated.

Grinding and Sharpening

Tools that are dull are worth no more than an old block with a split sheave. When someone confesses that he doesn't know how to sharpen tools and that he wants to learn, I'm full of sympathy. If he asks where to go to get them sharpened, I'm saddened; for there is no place close enough unless you have let out one corner of your shop to someone who can do it and is always there, and even that is like having someone to tie your shoelaces. The whole idea is something like writing with a sharp pencil: The lead may always be showing, but if you want a fine line, the pencil goes back to the sharpener every few minutes.

Most new tools come ground to the correct bevel, but only some of them are sharpened as well. There is a distinction here. When your tools need grinding, if this is beyond your capabilities, take them to a machine shop; for grinding is a once-in-a-while thing. Sharpening is putting a cutting edge on the bevel; it is a rather frequent thing and really not all that difficult. There are two methods of sharpening, and we'll discuss the old tried-and-true one first.

A power grinding wheel develops so much heat in the tool that if the bevel were brought to a fine edge, the very thinness of the metal would permit overheating and the temper would be destroyed. To prevent this, we hand-rub the tool on a sharpening stone. Keep the face of the stone lubricated with oil; it prevents the ground-off steel and stone particles from filling the pores in the stone. Sharpening oil can be purchased or made up as a 50/50 mixture of kerosene and cutting oil for hand threading. The latter is available at any hardware store.

Wanting to accomplish our purpose as quickly as possible, we start with a coarse stone to bring the tool to a sharp edge, and then switch to a finer stone to smooth it. By the end of this operation, there will be a "wire edge" that you can feel on the side opposite the bevel. The next step is to switch to a hard, very smooth stone, such as a hard Arkansas, and use it to polish the bevel edge. The wire edge on the side opposite the bevel will still be there, but one or two passes with the back of the tool flat on the stone will remove most of it. The edge is now stropped on an old-fashioned razor strop or an oil-soaked piece of leather tacked to the workbench. ("Stropping" means passing alternate sides of the cutting edge over the leather to remove all traces of the wire edge.) You should now be able to shave your arm with the tool or cleanly slice a piece of newspaper without tearing it. A trial cut on a piece of pine should leave an almost polished wood surface. Any whiter streaks or spots indicate duller areas on the edge, and you'll have to go back to the hard Arkansas and strop again to remove these.

You can rub chisels over the stone back and forth, or with a rotary motion; take care to maintain the same bevel at all times. Gouges are more difficult: you must rock the tool from side to side as well as back and forth, so as to sharpen the whole bevel evenly. Be careful on the corners to keep the cutting edge a straight line; don't round them. Shaped "slips" are used to touch up the inside edges.

If all this sounds involved and you want to invest in power tools, there is a new sharpening system that is easier, quicker, and more accurate. This system is the Woodcraft Mark II, available from the Woodcraft Supply Company in Woburn, Massachusetts. It involves grinding with aluminum-oxide cloth belts in varying grades, and it produces little heat build-up, an advantage over the grinding-wheel method. After grinding, the tool is honed on a buffing wheel charged with white rouge, which produces the final edge and polishes the tool. This system is expensive unless there is a great quantity of sharpening to be done, but it is an ideal setup.

Several tool catalogs also list the modern version of the old-fashioned whetstone. Nowadays, the wheel is turned over so that you can grind your tools on the flat face rather than on the rim of the stone. These wheels turn slowly (500 rpm) and are water-cooled. They also are powered by an electric motor, so you don't need a boy to turn the crank.

If you have an electric motor that you can attach a buffing wheel to, it will eliminate the final honing and stropping steps from your hand-sharpening system. This is a great time saver, as these two steps should be repeated whenever tools begin to dull. Grinding and rough sharpening should only be done to remove nicks in the cutting edge or to bring the bevel down after many sharpenings.

How do you tell that a tool is getting dull? By feel—is it getting harder to push? By the cut surface of the wood—is it no longer smooth and almost polished? By the wood fibers—are they tearing instead of being sheared off cleanly in end-grain cutting? Keep the edges honed, and you will do a better job of carving.

What to Look For, and Where

For historical background and design ideas, see the following books at the library or bookstores:

American Figureheads and Their Carvers, by Pauline A. Pinckney. W.W. Norton & Company; New York, NY. 1940.

Ships' Figureheads, by Peter Norton. Barre Publishing; Barre, MA. 1976.

Silent Pilots: Figureheads in the Mystic Seaport Museum, by Georgia W. Hamilton. Mystic Seaport Museum; Mystic, CT. 1984.

Old Ship Figureheads & Sterns, by H.G. Carr Laughton. Minton, Balch, & Co.; New York, NY. 1925.

Figureheads: Carving on Ships from Ancient Times to Twentieth Century, by Giancarlo Costa. Nautical Publishing Co.; Lymington, England. 1981.

The Arts of the Sailor, by Hervey Garrett Smith. Funk & Wagnalls; New York, NY. 1953.

The Decorative Arts of the Mariner, edited by Gervis Frere-Cook. Little, Brown & Co.; Boston, MA. 1966.

American Nautical Art and Antiques, by Jacqueline L. Kranz. Crown Publishers; New York, NY. 1975.

Grinling Gibbons and the English Woodcarving Tradition, by Frederick Oughton. Stobart; London, England. 1979.

The Marlinspike Sailor, by Hervey Garrett Smith. John deGraff, Inc.; Tuckahoe, NY. 1971.

Practical Woodcarving and Gilding, by Wheeler and Hayward. Evans Brothers, Ltd.; London, England. 1970.

Shipcarvers of North America, by M. V. Brewington. Barre Publishing Co.; Barre, MA. 1962.

For bird designs and colors, these books are a great help:

The American Eagle in Art and Design, by C.P. Horning. Dover Publications; New York, NY. 1978.

Audubon Water Bird Guide, by R.H. Pough. Doubleday; Garden City, NY. 1957.

The Ducks, Geese & Swans of North America, by F.H. Kortright. Stackpole; New York, NY. 1962.

Game Bird Carving, by B. Burk. Winchester Press; New York, NY. 1972.

For tools, try your local hardware and art supply stores, look in the Yellow Pages, or write for a catalog:

Garrett Wade Company, 161 Avenue of the Americas, New York, NY 10013 (send $4.00 for catalog).

Wood Carver's Supply, Inc., P.O. Box 8928, Norfolk, VA 23503 (free catalog).

Woodcraft Supply Corp., 41 Atlantic Ave., P.O. Box 4000, Woburn, MA 01888.

Frank Mittermeier, Inc., 3577 East Tremont Ave., Bronx, NY 10465–0002 (send $1.00 for catalog).

Highland Hardware, 1045 North Highland Ave. N.E., Atlanta, GA 30306 (send $1.00 for catalog).

Woodworker's Supply of New Mexico, 5604 Alameda Place N.E., Albuquerque, NM 87112 (free catalog).

The Fine Tool Shops, 170 West Rd., P.O. Box 7091, Portsmouth, NH 03801.

For wood, see your local boatyard, lumberyard, pattern shop, or furniture maker. If they don't have what you want, ask to see the catalogs of their suppliers.

For gold leaf and books of instruction, contact Art Essentials of New York Ltd., 3 Cross St., Suffern, NY 10901-4601.

For more on sharpening, I recommend you read *Home and Workshop Guide to Sharpening*, by Harry Walton. Popular Science Publishing Co.; New York, NY. 1967.

Full-sized plans and patterns for some of these carving projects have been drawn by the author for readers who prefer to work with them. A complete set of drawings includes alphabets, eagle, sea chest, billetheads, star, dolphin, feather, and oak leaf patterns. The price for the set is $24. Write WoodenBoat Plans, P.O. Box 78, Brooklin, ME 04616.

"It Ain't Easy"

And now, assuming with complete faith that you have arrived at this point without becoming discouraged, I can tell you a story about an elderly Maine boatbuilder whose competence I admire. Years ago, I saw a piece of work that he had produced that involved some masterly carving. Really wanting to know his technique for achieving such results, I asked him how he'd done it. After scratching his head for a minute and looking puzzled, he answered, "Wa'al...it ain't easy." I'll never be as skilled as he is, but I'm beginning to understand what he meant. You can't say, "Do thus and so, and this is what you'll get." Carving isn't like bolting two metal parts together. The first time you "do thus and so," the results may be disappointing—but after letting your hands become familiar with the tools for some time, you realize you are turning out something quite good. Consciously, you are not aware of doing anything different from the first time, but somewhere along the way, your hands have learned to translate to the wood what your imagination sees. So when your admiring friends ask, "How did you do it?" you, too, can answer, "It ain't easy."

Credits

Frontispiece:	Graham S. Hanna
Title page:	Benjamin Mendlowitz
Figure 1:	United States Naval Academy, Annapolis, Maryland (Model No. 55, H.H. Rogers Collection)
Figure 2:	Peabody Museum, Salem, Massachusetts
Figure 3:	Jack Whitehead
Figure 20 *(bottom left)*:	Steve Rubicam
Figure 46 *(top)*:	Marge Hanna
Figure 46 *(bottom)*:	Chesapeake Bay Maritime Museum, St. Michael's, Maryland
Figure 62:	Paul A. Darling
Figure 63:	Marge Hanna
Figure 65:	Graham S. Hanna
Figure 77:	William Thuss
Figure 78 *(top)*:	Marge Hanna
Figure 79:	Courtesy of Cliff Fremstad
Figure 83:	Benjamin Mendlowitz
Figure 84:	Marty Loken

All carvings and photos are by the author unless otherwise noted.